CORRUPTION

FRAUD, EMBEZZLEMENT AND OTHER BAD ACTS AND THE AUDITORS THAT FOUND THEM

GREGORY P. HAWKINS
LONN LITCHFIELD

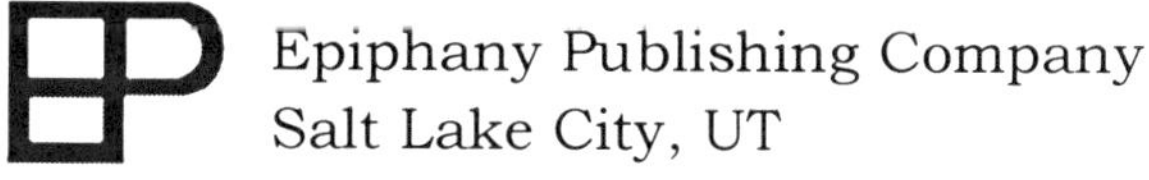

Disclaimer: In writing this book, we have tried to be factually accurate and we have relied on sources that are generally reliable, such as audit reports and newspaper articles, but it is possible that some facts do not turn out to be accurate. It is not our intent to damage anyone and we bear no ill will toward anyone in this book, including those who we report have been convicted of crimes or that have had a hand in what we label corrupt or culpable behavior. Our intent is to use the stories to illustrate our ideas about the nature of government corruption and how auditors help eliminate it. Ultimately, this book sets out our opinions, which do not rest on any of these stories.

Epiphany Publishing Company
Salt Lake City, Utah

ISBN 978-0-9849528-4-7

Library of Congress Control Number: 2014935337

TABLE OF CONTENTS

INTRODUCTION
APPLES AND ORANGES
LONN LITCHFIELD

It is regrettable that *audit* has become a scary word. The response to, "I'm here to audit you," is usually a feeling of dread. This is unfortunate because audits, done right, are a powerful tool for ensuring that government, or any organization, meets its objectives. They save governments millions of dollars, they secure liberty, and they help eliminate corruption.

Publically, people in power often praise auditors. They extol transparency in government. They gush about the importance of audit reports. But usually this is just lip service. The reality is that auditors are rarely welcome. Very few of those in government will cheer when the auditor arrives. Responses range from mild annoyance to open hostility to stonewalling. While auditors save millions of dollars, help eliminate corruption, and secure liberty, they are most often unappreciated.

Additionally, auditors are almost always underfunded. And by "almost always" we mean that we are not aware of a single example of government auditors being adequately funded, but in such a large world, we are willing to concede that it may have happened somewhere at some time.

The term *audit,* for our purposes, means an objective evaluation of evidence related to established criteria. In other words, an auditor compares what happened in real life with what should have happened and reports the findings. In a government context, there are many people who have responsibilities that meet this definition, but they are not always called auditors. A comptroller, an accountant, a special counsel, or an inspector general may conduct an evaluation that fits the definition of an audit. So, too, could an investigator, a police officer, a county attorney, or a legislative aide.

It is difficult to measure the success of government actions. To a large degree, a corporation can measure its ultimate success by its profits. The term "the bottom line" actually refers to the place on accounting reports where the profits of a company are found. When costs are subtracted from revenues, the profits are written on the bottom line. Profits are a relatively clear, relatively objective, and unforgiving measure of all the business decisions that were made. Good decisions increase profits; bad decisions decrease profits. Decisions that don't affect profits one way or another probably don't matter much.

Governments do not have profits. The success or failure of a government has to be measured in a different way. Often, the success of government is measured by the work that is performed, but that is really only one consideration. Government actions begin with *policies,* ideas about what is right and what is wrong for a government to do. Policies lead to *objectives*, plans and strategies for implementing the policies. *Government actions*, the work, attempt to meet the objectives. Finally, there are the results, the effect of the government activities.

Policy ➔ Objectives ➔ Government Action (Work) ➔ Results

If the results are not as anticipated, it could be because the work was not done, because the objectives were not met, or because the policies were wrong. Results have to be measured for government to improve. Are the results those that were intended when the policy was adopted, the objective set, and the government action decided upon?

The word ***corruption*** means that something is changed, degraded, or debased, either intentionally or by error, to a condition different from what was intended in its creation. When the results are not as anticipated, we find corruption. The corruption may be in the policy, the objectives, or the work. When the policy, objectives, or work result in a condition that is different from the intended outcome, we meet the definition of corruption.

There is a difference between ***corruption*** and ***culpability***. While corruption is a condition that is debased from what was intended, culpability is about intention, fault, blame, liability and accountability. Something—such as a government program, an employee, or a policy—may be corrupt even if no one is at fault or to blame.

When we think of corruption, we usually think of culpable corruption, such as fraud, theft, bribery, or nepotism. But often, non–culpable corruption is more damaging than culpable corruption. No one is thinking evil thoughts, no one is trying to do harm, but the purposes for which the government is established are not accomplished. Hearts are right, intentions are good, but there are problematic results. Whether the corruption is culpable or not, it needs to be addressed. Understanding the difference between corruption and culpability is important in eliminating corruption. Consider the following illustration.

Imagine a beautiful apple. It is juicy and delicious. It crunches when you bite into it. The skin is thin and chewy. Its color is rich and inviting. It is symmetrical and well–formed. The purpose of an apple is to be eaten and everything about the apple makes you want to eat it. This perfect apple is uncorrupted.

But would you eat an apple that is filled with razorblades and poisons? Such an apple is, by definition, corrupt: it is has been changed so that it is not suitable for eating. Filling an apple with razorblades and poisons requires a person to intentionally misbehave. Someone is culpable for corrupting the apple, but we do not know who it was. But you don't have to determine who is to blame to know that you don't want to eat the apple. The primary conclusion is "don't eat the apple." Who is to blame is secondary.

A smashed apple is also uninviting. Although it is possible that someone intentionally crushed it, it is also possible that it simply smashed when it fell out of the tree. We cannot say who did it, and we cannot even say if anyone did it. But the question of whether someone is at fault is not relevant to our determination not to eat the apple. Again, the primary determination is that the apple is corrupt; culpability is secondary.

You wouldn't eat a rotten apple either. Apples become corrupt over time. You don't even think about fault. You simply don't eat the apple. Similarly, an apple can be inedible because it grew stunted and twisted. Should we blame someone for a malformed apple? It is a ridiculous question.

Rotten apples and corrupt governments can be similar in one respect. With apples, you don't have to establish blame to know that the apple can't be eaten. With government it is not always necessary to determine who is to blame to know that something—the policy, the objectives, or the work—needs to be fixed. For auditors, identifying corruption is primary; identifying culpability is secondary. This understanding and approach has been reduced to the practical maxims:

Focus on bad apples, not bad people.
Fix the problem, not the blame.

Government auditors, in particular, should primarily focus on corruption and only secondarily on culpability. This does not mean culpability should be ignored, but culpability is usually within the jurisdiction of someone else in the government. Because of an auditor's findings, Human Resources may need to fire somebody, but that is not the auditor's role. The prosecuting attorney may need to bring criminal charges, but that is not the auditor's role. Government officers or managers may need to conduct better training or implement better internal controls, but that is not the auditor's role. Voters may not re–elect an elected official to office, but that is not the auditor's role. The auditor's role is to identify the corruption and its cause—which may include identifying the individuals that are accountable—and to communicate the finding to those who are empowered to resolve the problem, or who are accountable for doing nothing.

Non–culpable corruption can be more of a problem than culpable corruption. There are dozens of examples, but consider the following illustration.

A government manager needs to use some oranges that are on a table down the hall. To make good decisions, she needs to know how many oranges are available. The success of the organization depends on the manager's decisions. The sooner the manager makes decisions the better. The manager asks an employee to go down the hall and count the oranges and tell her how many there are. The employee has several options for responding to this assignment.

- Option 1: the employee walks down the hall, comes back and reports that there are ten oranges.
- Option 2: the employee walks down the hall, reports that there are ten oranges and asks, "Is there anything else I can help with?"
- Option 3: the employee reports that there are ten oranges and asks, "Is there anything else I can do? I could find out where we got the oranges, how much they cost, or whether we will receive more oranges in the future."
- Option 4: the employee walks down the hall and thinks, "the manager doesn't know how many oranges there are." The employee takes two oranges and promptly reports that there are

eight oranges.

- Option 5: the employee takes two oranges, but to hide his tracks, he waits a week before he reports that there are eight oranges. During that time, the oranges spoil, leaving only six in the basket.
- Option 6: the employee counts the oranges and returns to his office. He decides to write a report about oranges for the manager. He's positively gleeful when he thinks about how much the manager is going to love his report. He gathers information about nearby stores that sell oranges, different varieties of oranges, the historical price trends of oranges, an interesting anecdote about oranges in the court of Louis XIV, attempts by poets to rhyme with "orange." But it is a big project and after a couple of weeks his attention has shifted elsewhere. He never delivers the report, nor even the count to the manager. In the meantime, all ten oranges rot and are lost.

Option 1 is good and adequate. The task was performed as intended when it was assigned. The employee fulfilled the task and the manager could make the decisions. But Option 2 is better and more helpful than Option 1. Option 3 is better still. No corruption can be found in any of these options.

The behavior of the employee in Option 4 in taking two of the oranges was both corrupt and culpable. The manager did not have as many oranges as she should and the decisions she could make are more limited than they would have been with ten oranges. This is not the condition that was intended. And the condition was created by conduct that was inappropriate, wrong, punishable, and even evil. But the manager still had eight oranges and had information she could use to make decisions.

Option 5 involves behavior that was both more corrupt and more culpable than Option 4 because the employee delayed getting the information to the manager. Besides stealing two oranges, he also delayed the manager's ability to make any decision.

But compare Option 4 and Option 5 with Option 6. Despite the best intentions of the employee, the manager never had the information she needed to make good decisions and the resources she needed were lost. The manager never got the information, the manager never made decisions, and all the resources were lost. Intentions were good, but the result was horrible. Although there is certainly blame and fault, there is no intentional harm. There is no culpability in Option 6, but Option 6 is corrupt and the organization failed to accomplish its objectives. Option 6 is even more damaging to the organization than Option 5. Although there is no culpability in Option 6, it is more corrupt than Option 5. Corruption needs to be eliminated even if it is not culpable.

In the stories in this book, government auditors—regardless of their formal titles—identify corruption, measure it, and report what they find to the people and to those in power. In most of these stories, there is someone who is clearly culpable. But in many of these stories there are others who, although they were not culpable, had the authority and opportunity to prevent the corruption from happening in the first place. They were too busy, or too underfunded, or too trusting, to eliminate or prevent the corruption. When an auditor identifies corruption, corruption can be reduced and often eliminated.

The Declaration of Independence of the United States affirms that governments are instituted to secure life, liberty, and the pursuit of happiness. To the degree a government in the United States fails to secure these rights, it is corrupt. Auditors identify corruption, measure it, and make recommendations to eliminate it. To the extent government corruption is eliminated, liberty is protected and strengthened. Auditors are always essential and always increase liberty.

Audits provide essential accountability and transparency over government programs. Given the current challenges facing governments and their programs, the oversight provided through auditing is more critical than ever. Government auditing provides objective analysis and information needed to make the decisions necessary to help create a better future.

— Comptroller General of the United States,
Government Auditing Standards 2011

CHAPTER 1
SODUS, NEW YORK, USA

The Town of Sodus is located in upstate New York, just about two miles inland from the southern shore of Lake Ontario. Sandwiched between Highway 104 on the north and Highway 88 on the south, this tiny community is surrounded by bucolic fields and orchards that provide produce for roadside stands and for the town's local farm market, which is held weekly during good weather in the parking lot behind the Red Brick Church on Main Street. Other main attractions include sledding and skiing at Brantling Ski Center, hiking at Beechwood State Park and dining at Bubba's Roadhouse, a family-owned bar and restaurant. Statistically, Sodus is a very unexceptional little town—at least it was—until the day that Town Clerk Linda Verhow decided to start helping herself to its limited resources.

In March of 2010, state police arrested Verhow and charged her with second–degree grand larceny, a Class C felony. A seemingly ordinary, middle–aged town employee, Verhow had used her trusted position in the town office to embezzle more than $50,000 from her friends, neighbors, and work associates. Verhow was no stranger to this small upstate rural community. She had served as the deputy clerk of the town from 1989 to 2004. Accepting the town clerk position in 2004 was not really a huge leap for someone who had already proved herself to be friendly, competent, and efficient.

Following her resignation in September of 2009, the town initiated a six–month investigation conducted by the Wayne County District Attorney's office, state police, and the state Comptroller's office. It was not until Verhow learned of the anticipated audit of the town books that she was ready to confess to eight years' worth of fraud, starting as far back as 2002.

The people of Sodus were stunned. How could such brazen thievery happen in a small community where the average crime rate is no more than an assault, a car theft and a few burglaries a year? Until now, the town had been governed by Steven LeRoy, supervisor and chief fiscal officer, and four other elected officials without any serious incidents. Once the audit report brought her shady dealings out into the light, the next perplexing question on everyone's mind was, "How could someone we have known and trusted for years betray us in such a cold and calculating manner?"

Profile of an Embezzler

Embezzlement is defined as the fraudulent appropriation of money or property entrusted to one's care but belonging to someone else. Each year in the United States, millions of dollars are stolen or misappropriated from public funds of local and state organizations. Town and county clerks, sheriffs, treasurers, public utilities directors, municipal office holders, and school personnel have all been caught stealing from their local communities. In most cases, the crime has not been a one–time event but a prolonged series of illegal activity spanning months or even years, as was the case with Linda Verhow.

After prostitution, embezzlement is the only other criminal activity that is perpetrated more by women than by men. According to Marquet International, a Boston consulting firm, the average embezzler is in her late forties and has no previous criminal record. She is in mid–level management or accounting and highly trusted. Customers and associates will describe her as well–spoken, likeable and courteous, but they will probably also admit that they really don't know her very well because there seems to be an invisible wall around her. At some level, embezzlement requires an almost sociopathic lack of conscience and a total disregard for the damage being done to innocent victims. For Linda Verhow, stealing from the little town of Sodus became a process of manipulation and control, one she fully expected to execute without fear of exposure—that is, until the auditors came to town.

Embezzlement is an interesting crime in that while almost 80 percent of these kinds of fraud cases are committed by women, they tend to take only about 20 percent of the money. Unlike men, who steal to "look good" in the eyes of their peers and to maintain a lavish lifestyle, women embezzlers are often motivated by the need to provide for themselves and their family, to satisfy an addiction such as gambling, alcohol, or drugs, or to cover compulsive shopping habits based on deep psychological or emotional needs. Although they have average or above–average intelligence, they lack the ability to predict the consequences of their actions. As Dana Turner, security practitioner for Security Education Systems of San Antonio explains, "Although they say they'll only do it (steal) once and then put it back, the instant gratification from solving their financial problems is a powerful force, making embezzlement one of the most habitual crimes there is, even more so than child molesting or serial killing." Each time they avoid detection, perpetrators become more convinced that they will never get caught because they have outsmarted everyone.

Enter the Auditor

As soon as Linda Verhow learned that the town clerk's books were going to be officially examined by a professional team, she confessed to her crime and immediately repaid $17,053. The auditing process would, however, reveal that she had taken much more. According to the final report, a total of $53,148 had been stolen from the Tax Collector's Account, the Water Account, and the Town Clerk's Account, all of which were under her control during this time period.

Uncovering the Embezzler's Method of Operation

Part of Verhow's scheme involved placing money in the town safe during the day and then stealing it back at night. She created false deposit tickets to hide the losses. As town clerk, Verhow also took cash tax payments, failed to record them and then charged interest and late penalties, which would be used to replace some of the cash that she had taken. Money was siphoned from licenses, permits, water–bill payments, office fees, and property and school taxes. If one of the three town accounts became suspiciously low, Verhow temporarily shifted funds to cover the discrepancy. Her strategy seemed foolproof to her, but it was not.

As part of her job, Linda Verhow dutifully prepared monthly reports for the supervisor. However, no one seemed to mind that the monthly reports admitted that deposits were not always turned in on time. Neither did anyone consider the value of occasionally checking Verhow's statements against actual bank balances, records, receipts, canceled checks, or check images. The board limited its involvement to reviewing her manufactured monthly and yearly statements.

Because Verhow had full access to computerized billing and records, she was free to adjust financial numbers without raising suspicions from anyone. Although the board also had full access to all financial transactions and applications, they had no comprehensive policies or procedures for guarding the integrity of the town clerk position and little interest in assuming this responsibility.

Uncovering the Crime

The team sent out by Albany's Comptroller, Thomas P. DiNapoli, interviewed the supervisor and other local officials. They counted all moneys in all accounts. They found old, un–cashed checks hidden carelessly in desk drawers. Later, they discovered that at least two taxpayers had been double–charged and fined for late payments as a way to fund Verhow's stealing. They compared journal receipts and deposits for discrepancies. Likewise, they compared monthly reports with source documents. They scrutinized disbursements from all three accounts over which Verhow had control. They even studied Wayne County's tax records. Examiners followed the strict Generally Accepted Government Auditing Standard (GAGAS) guidelines. The final conclusion was that, over an eight–year period, Linda Verhow had systematically embezzled more than $50,000 from the Town of Sodus.

Truth and Consequences

While the people of Sodus initially reacted with disbelief, as reality set in so did outrage and a sense of betrayal. The auditor's report not only spelled out the extent of the crime but also detailed how Verhow had been able to disguise her illegal actions for so long. Additionally, it offered important measures that could be taken to prevent any future misappropriation of funds. Practical suggestions included performing thorough, annual audits of the books; developing an information technology policy and limiting access to the electronic records; insisting that all moneys and deposits be made in a timely manner; documenting receipts and keeping copies on file; independently examining and reviewing records periodically; reconciling bank statements monthly; and accurately recording and documenting all money transactions. The auditors also strongly recommended trying to recover as much of the $53,148 as possible from the perpetrator.

Steven LeRoy and his board took the recommendations of the audit very seriously. Sobered by this unpleasant experience, they immediately moved to put in place important safeguards, policies and procedures. LeRoy expressed his town's appreciation when he said, "We want to thank your entire group for their professional completion of this audit. The team was very understanding and helpful during an extremely stressful time for our entire municipal staff."

Never marry for money. Ye'll borrow it cheaper.

— Scottish Proverb

CHAPTER 2

NASHVILLE-DAVIDSON COUNTY, TENNESSEE, USA

C.S. Lewis makes an interesting observation in his famous satire *The Screwtape Letters*. "Indeed the safest road to Hell is the gradual one—the gentle slope, soft underfoot, without sudden turnings, without milestones, without sign posts." In truth, it is often a series of small, seemingly insignificant decisions that can become the undoing of an otherwise successful career. In 2012, John Arriola, County Clerk of Nashville–Davidson County, would find this to be true for his own life experience, and it would be Jim Arnette, Director for the Division of County Audit, who would uncover those telltale "minor" mistakes that would eventually lead to Arriola's disgraced resignation.

A Little Bit Country

John Arriola was born, bred, and educated in Nashville, Tennessee. After graduating from the University of Tennessee at Martin, he worked in various healthcare–related businesses in the area. He also served as a State Representative from 1990–2002. Prior to winning the election for the County Clerk position, he served as

Vice President of the Nashville Memorial Hospital. He also owned the popular Norman Couser's Country Cooking Restaurant, which his parents operated. Arriola is married to Michelle, a two–time board member of the Metro Council, and they have two beautiful daughters. It would seem like the perfect life.

However, in 2011, Nashville Mayor Karl Dean requested that the state conduct an audit of Office of the County Clerk to look specifically at two areas of concern: cash management procedures and contracts and procurement procedures. Too many complaints were flying around to be ignored any longer. It didn't take long to uncover weak internal controls, lack of clear–cut policies and sloppy handling of finances. However, what really lit the fuse was the discovery that Arriola had made an additional $120,000 in the years 2006–2011 in an unusual way. In addition to the standard $40 marriage license fee, he had been charging an extra $40 to marry couples at his office. His personal fee was always collected in cash and never mentioned on the books. While it would have been perfectly legal for the County Clerk to accept any gratuities offered by grateful couples, the act of charging a fee and calling it a gratuity was not at all legal. It was corruption.

Because Arriola made the marriage documentation requirements as flexible as possible, almost 3,000 couples, many of them betrothed immigrants, flocked to the County Office during those five years. In fact, eventually Fridays were set aside by the County Clerk's Office for the specific purpose of conducting marriages. Couples were herded through, back–to–back. Each time, $40 in cash was deposited in an envelope and handed to Arriola. While he would later deny that he ever charged this fee, sworn testimony from office employees would indicate otherwise.

The marriage fee scandal may have been the smoking gun, but the auditor's thorough work uncovered several other discrepancies and deficiencies as well. The fact that Arriola did not require his employees to maintain time and attendance records fostered corruption. In 2009, 63 employees were paid $21,000 for overtime that they did not work. The next year, an additional $1,136.98 was paid to some of the part–time employees who thought their bigger paychecks were simply bonuses for work well done. Two other part–time employees had work–hours deducted without any explanatory documentation. Most full–time employees were under the impression that they were not required to work a 40–hour week because they were on salary. Employees were allowed to draw against their annual paid leave, sick leave, and compensatory time before earning it. At least one part–time employee was inappropriately receiving full–time benefits of paid leave and health insurance.

Then there was the problem of conflicts of interests. In 2006, Arriola gave long–time friend Susan Andrews and her PR firm, Andrews Agency, a no–bid contract for $16,826. The part–time campaign manager and outreach coordinator did not keep a record of hours worked, was not supervised and took time off for vacations and illness with full pay. The total bill for five years was only $63,085, but during that time, not one outreach report was generated or completed on behalf of the County Clerk. The fact that Arriola hired a person who was renting a home from him as a seasonal employee without disclosing the relationship did not look good either. It was corrupt.

Requiring employees to conduct campaign activities during office hours was another form of corruption. Sworn testimony from employees indicated they were expected to participate in re–election fundraising activities even during their normal work hours and sometimes at the County Clerk's Office. On occasion they would leave work early to help with a fundraiser, but they would never be docked in their paychecks. The auditor also noticed that John Arriola seemed to have no qualms about spending taxpayer money inappropriately to promote himself as a brand either. Consider the $806 studio portrait he commissioned or the $4,800 John Arriola logo or the $34,027 he spent replacing generic County Clerk signs with those with his own name added.

It has been said that when the federal government could not make charges stick against Al Capone, the IRS did. The auditor's report to the Metro Council would also open that box for County Clerk John Arriola. Although he had appropriated a $33,000 SUV Tahoe for commuting from home to work, Arriola kept no mileage records to be reported to the Metro Finance Dept. As a result, this benefit was not included on his W 2 forms. There would also be all those cash marriage–fee payments to consider.

During the summer of 2011, District Attorney General Torry Johnson requested that the Federal Bureau of Investigation become involved. Suspecting that the axe was about to fall, Arriola quickly instituted many improvements in policy and procedure at the County Clerk's Office. However, it was a case of too little too late. The auditor's final draft was submitted to the Metro Council in January of 2012. Arriola used his recent office adjustments as a defense against some of the charges. He also repeatedly maintained that the County Clerk was not legally bound to the policies and procedures of the Metro Government.

While it was true that the County Clerk's Office had some liberty to operate independently, the lack of any written personnel policies and procedures in Arriola's office resulted in confusion about what was and was not acceptable behavior for all those concerned. The auditor stressed that such clearly defined policies would help ensure compliance and facilitate record keeping. Time and attendance records should be kept and signed by each employee. Furthermore, leave records should be forwarded to Metro Finance so that they could be included in the Comprehensive Annual Financial Report of the Metro Government. Because of the lack of internal controls over collections, the County Clerk's Office was highly vulnerable to funds being misappropriated, lost, or stolen.

Although the Metro Council began calling for his resignation in February of 2012, shortly after the auditor's report had been accepted, John Arriola hung on until June. It appears that his resignation may have been tied to an agreement to close the investigation into possible criminal activity. Coinciding with Arriola's resignation, the Bureau dropped further involvement in the case.

Although it has never been established that Arriola was culpable, at least the corruption has ended. Interim County Clerk Brenda Wynn was easily re–elected in November, when Arriola's term officially expired, she became the first African–American to win any election for a Davidson County constitutional office. Today, weddings are performed as a free public service for residents of Davidson County. Wynn has worked to build a cooperative relationship between her office and the rest of Metro Government. Records are kept and internal controls are in place. The last remaining problem is what to do with $34,000 worth of County Clerk signs with the wrong name on them.

Now you understand. Anything goes wrong, anything at all—your fault, my fault, nobody's fault—it don't matter—I'm gonna blow your head off. It's as simple as that.

— John Wayne, *Big Jake*

CHAPTER 3

ORANGE COUNTY, CALIFORNIA, USA

Government corruption comes in different sizes and different flavors. A cashier steals from the cash drawer. A contractor charges $600 for a toilet seat. A city council puts the money and the accounting in the same hands. A relative is paid a salary and never comes to work.

But the biggest corruption is completely, 100%, totally legal.

When the Voters Give You a Lemon . . .

Robert Citron was a six–term Treasurer of wealthy Orange County, California. He was respected and trusted, with a dignified legacy and retirement coming up. Late in Citron's career, California's Proposition 13 changed the game on him a little bit. When he changed himself in response, the audit and inspection response was weak. Due to the trust Citron had accumulated, he was left largely to his own devices.

Prop 13 made it illegal to raise property taxes to balance county budgets. Orange County residents, at the same time, wished to continue benefitting from their court systems, public sanitation, welfare, library systems, county hospitals, parks, and roads. They showed no interest in tightening their belts on any of these services. After all, don't we pay politicians to come up with ways to provide the services we demand without making us pay taxes?

Citron thought. And he tapped his chin. And he thought some more. And when he had thought for a while, he ran for re–election promising the same robust county services without raising taxes. He proposed to generate increased county revenue not through taxes, but by using public money to play the markets.

The typical U.S. county generates about 61% of its revenue through property, sales, and other taxes. It receives another 33% or so from its parent state and gets another 3% from the federal government. Three percent comes from other sources.

Orange County, however, already had the legal right to generate income through bond revenue, that is, by borrowing money. In Orange County, they parlayed this borrowing right far beyond simple interest–bearing bonds; Citron developed a plan for investing in "interest–rate derivative contracts." Put simply, these contracts allow investors to bet for or against increases in the interest rates offered by the Federal Reserve. This use of public money was risky. It required a high degree of sophistication. And Citron's plan required leveraging, effectively borrowing money to make bigger bets.

. . . Make Lemonade!

And what happened to these bets, you might ask? Citron's bets paid off. Beautiful! For a while, the investment returns rolled in, and the county looked great. Wealthy Orange County residents enjoyed the services to which they were accustomed, and Prop 13 seemed like little more than a distant annoyance.

Later, in the postmortem, Dale Scott, a San Francisco financial advisor to local governments, summarized Orange County's bankruptcy neatly: "You can pin this almost 100 percent on Proposition 13. The only reason people are out there trying to turn two dimes into a quarter is they can't finance basic needs anyway else. The Music Man comes in and says, 'I can get you 10 percent when everyone else gets 5 percent,' and he's a hero."

As the investment returns rolled in, Citron stacked and leveraged the bets higher and higher. Other local governments, such as school boards, jumped on the bandwagon. More and more politicians got on board the gravy train. Orange County's annual budgets were in the $3.7 billion range at that time, with $462 million in discretionary funds for 1994–1995. Over 35% of that discretionary fund came from investment income.

Citron managed accounts worth $8 billion and leveraged the county's money at ratios of 1.5 to 2.9. We're not talking about an audit that failed to catch a grandma filching $100 grand from the cash drawer. We're talking about risking the entire infrastructure of a county with 3 million residents. At that point, a system of checks–and–balances is no longer optional. There is a lot at stake, and your audit system better have fangs down to its chin.

Sweet or Sour?

The moment that U.S. interest rates turned the wrong way, Orange County went awash in debt. Its losses eventually soared over $2 billion. In February 1994, as the first bill collectors came banging at the door, Citron made the county's margin payments by issuing a colossal $600 million bond—more borrowed money.

The punch line is, even as Citron was borrowing so much to cover Orange County's devastating losses, various smaller bureaucracies with money in the investment fund plowed more money into the bets. Organizations such as the Orange County Board of Education, the

Irvine Unified School District, the Newport–Mesa Unified School District, and the North Orange County Community College District borrowed a total of $200 million more to invest in Citron's funds.

So, what is the worst that can happen when a government stops delivering public services and starts acting like an investment fund? It includes laid–off government workers, unpaid welfare checks, uncollected garbage, collapsing county government, and years of rebuilding.

But when Orange County went under, Murphy's Law fully took hold. Orange County could not obtain assistance from California state government because Democrats were in the majority and they had little interest in helping out a mega–rich, mega–white, mega–conservative county just south of L.A. The delicious irony: Bob Citron was the only notable Democratic politician in Orange County.

Orange County declared bankruptcy. Robert Citron pleaded guilty to six felonies, including lying to those who had bought into his investment funds, but there was no allegation that the extremely risky transactions he engaged in on behalf of Orange County were unlawful. Orange County cut every budget project, laid off around 3,000 public employees, and reduced all services. Citron got five years' probation and 1000 hours of community service. His legacy of public service was destroyed.

Citron's culpability was not the cause of the corruption that bankrupted Orange County. Citron corrupted Orange County government by participating in a highly speculative and highly volatile market. He apparently did so mostly legally. And he did so with the approval of the voters and other politicians. Not surprisingly, neither state law nor county ordinance provided for independent reviews of Citron's speculations. The corruption that led to the most spectacular downfall of a local government in United States history was not even illegal.

Thou shalt not kill.
Thou shalt not commit adultery.
Thou shalt not steal.
Thou shalt not bear false witness against thy neighbour.
Thou shalt not covet thy neighbour's house, thou shalt not covet thy neighbour's wife, nor his manservant, nor his maidservant, nor his ox, nor his ass, nor any thing that is thy neighbour's.

— Exodus 20:15–17 (KJV)

CHAPTER 4

SALT LAKE COUNTY, UTAH, USA

In the fall of 2011, Michelle Benward walked into the Human Resources Division of Salt Lake County and said, "One of your employees killed my sister." Everyone was listening.

Her sister, Jami Christiansen, was an attractive, 38–year–old woman who had struggled with mental health issues since childhood. She had engaged in a sexual relationship with Richard Parks, a 64–year–old who ran Salt Lake County's AmeriCorps program. Years previously, Parks had been Christiansen's teacher and more recently, Christiansen was an AmeriCorps volunteer in a program run by Parks, but located 300 miles away in St. George, Washington

County, Utah.

HR referred the case first to the District Attorney, who determined that there was no evidence to link Parks to Christiansen's death. The District Attorney also determined that the sexual relationship was consensual and that Parks was not guilty of any sexual impropriety, although the inappropriate nature of the affair led to serious questions about Parks' professional judgment and the way he'd been doing his job.

During the investigation, Benward gave her late sister's email login and password to HR. HR found an email from Parks to Christiansen in which he instructed her to fabricate several months of missing time cards. HR turned the case over to Salt Lake County Auditor Gregory P. Hawkins.

When Saw We Thee a Stranger, and Took Thee In?

A small community of religious fundamentalist straddles the Utah–Arizona border. North of the line, the town is known as Hildale; the Arizona side is called Colorado City. There, the Fundamentalist Church of Jesus Christ of Latter–day Saints practices polygamy and owns all property in common. FLDS leaders are as harsh as the rocky desert all around. They exercise supreme control over all aspects of life. They arrange the polygamist marriages, sometimes between very mature men and teenage women. They dictate standards of dress and hairstyles. If someone disagrees or disobeys, they are declared an "apostate," they lose their spouses and children, they are stripped of their physical possessions, and they are exiled from the community.

Some of the "apostates" who find themselves driven out of the community include boys as young as thirteen. Their crimes? Watching movies, surfing the Internet, playing video games, and flirting with, talking to, or simply looking at girls. There's another, even more sinister reason as well: sending these boys away reduces the competition for available women. FLDS leaders simply turn out these "lost boys," their own children and grandchildren and nephews and cousins, and leave them to fend for themselves, thrust out into "Babylon." Through no fault of their own, they are thrust out into the world, alone, penniless, with no education and no skills. The Lost Boys find themselves in a sympathetic situation and many people in the area support helping them establish new lives.

AmeriCorps is the domestic equivalent of the Peace Corps. Programs are operated by charitable organizations and staffed by volunteers. The volunteers are paid a monthly stipend of around $1,000 per month and, if they complete a year of service and meet the requirements of the program, they receive a tuition voucher. The money for the program comes from the federal government to state and local governments, who ensure that the federal program is operated according to the rules. Although it is difficult to establish the events that led Salt Lake County to operate an AmeriCorps program for the Lost Boys in far off St. George, it appears that several in the state government played roles. The thought seemed to be that Salt Lake County knew how to operate an AmeriCorps program.

Funding for a program to help the Lost Boys was the result of the combined efforts of two local non–profit organizations: New Frontiers for Families and the Diversity Foundation. They envisioned providing shelter and training for Lost Boys. After a great deal of lobbying, the home received additional assistance from the federal AmeriCorps program, which would provide funding for employees and volunteers to help out at the new facility.

Jeremy Johnson was a local businessman. Johnson offered to donate a house he owned in St. George for the Lost Boys program. The program moved in and operated for a few years, but Johnson never actually donated the house. Johnson has since had some interesting legal issues, but they are not too closely related to the Salt Lake County's AmeriCorps program. The home, called the House Just off Bluff, opened in the late summer of 2007.

Parks, the Salt Lake County administrator of AmeriCorps programs, arranged for Michelle Benward, a long–time family friend, to be appointed Clinical Director for the facility. Parks got Benward's sister Jami Christiansen a volunteer position at the House.

It was a promising beginning.

House upon Sand

Over a period of several months, the plight of the Lost Boys drew national attention. At last, a "dirty little secret" was being exposed, and for a while, it seemed that the program would attract more in the way of resources and financial assistance. But the program was riddled with corruption.

Some of the corruption was not culpable—it is difficult to operate a program like the House Just Off Bluff from 300 miles away. Volunteers, especially Christiansen, were not held accountable for their work, or even their time. Often, they just didn't show up for work. Time cards, required for payments under the AmeriCorps rules, were not turned in, but there were no consequences. It was doubtful whether the Lost Boys were being helped at all.

But Parks was also taking advantage of the situation. Every few months he would take a trip to sunny St. George on Salt Lake County's dime. He would drop by the House, chat with the staff and volunteers, maybe run through a yoga session to teach the Lost Boys marketable skills. Then he and Christiansen would head for Mesquite, a party town just over the border in Nevada for a night of whatever, leaving the hotel in St. George that the County paid for unused.

For her part, Michelle Benward was violating AmeriCorps rules by acting as a volunteer while she was working as Clinical Director. And she was inappropriately counting as volunteer time her travel time from her home in Escalante, Utah, to St. George, about 175 miles away. Also, Benward had no current licenses, nor credentials for the job she was holding.

Benward's double dipping—which was actually triple dipping—and her lack of credentials was discovered in October of 2008. This by itself was against AmeriCorps policy, but that wasn't the worst of it. Neighbors had started complaining. It turned out that the House Just Off Bluff was not properly zoned for the purpose of sheltering at-risk youths. The arrangement with AmeriCorps was terminated, the House Just Off Bluff was forced to shut down, and Michelle Benward and her sister Jami Christiansen—along with other AmeriCorps members—lost their jobs.

Michelle kept in touch with her sister over the next eighteen months, and Jami continued to have mental health issues. Jami admitted that she had been having a sexual affair with her married former teacher and program administrator, Richard Parks. He had made the 300 mile journey from Salt Lake City at least four times in 2007 and 2008 while the House was in operation. By the time Jami turned up dead from a drug overdose, Michelle had come to the conclusion that her relationship with Richard Parks had not been entirely consensual—and that the affair had in one way or another led to Jami's apparent suicide.

Even though she herself had benefited from a number of shenanigans surrounding the House and the project, Michelle Benward decided to blow the whistle.

And the Rain Descended

When the Salt Lake County Auditor's office started looking into it, they found that Parks had been very sloppy in doing his job. Ultimately, over $95,000 was misappropriated. It was a clear case of fraud—and since the money in question had ultimately come from a federal program, the FBI was brought into the investigation.

The subsequent investigation revealed that Parks had:

- overpaid AmeriCorps members, falsifying records in order to do so;
- knowingly hired Michelle Benward as Clinical Director in violation of AmeriCorps policy;
- allowed Benward to report time spent commuting as "service hours;"
- either doctored time sheets and performance evaluations himself, or accepted them knowing they had been falsified;
- certified AmeriCorps members working at the house for "education credits" and awards when they had not fulfilled the necessary requirements;
- failed to take action when AmeriCorps members didn't turn in time sheets on schedule (in some cases, sheets had not been turned in for almost six months);
- paid AmeriCorps members "incentive bonuses" in order to get them to stay around, regardless of their performance;
- used AmeriCorps funds for personal reasons—in this case, paying for his trips to St. George in order to carry on his affair with Jami.

Oddly, except for the last item, Parks did not directly benefit from any of this. So why did he do it? Apparently, in order to keep his job. According to the auditor's report, Parks' employment was contingent upon continuation of that AmeriCorps funding, which was channeled through the Salt Lake County government. He had apparently also wanted to provide favors for old acquaintances—Michelle Benward and Jami Christiansen—regardless of their qualifications. Furthermore, his actions may have been justified in his own mind because this particular project was a relatively minor one, located in a small desert community hundreds of miles from anywhere. Who would notice?

In addition to motive and rationalization, there is a third element to be considered when it comes to any crime: opportunity. As is usually the case, the opportunity was provided by those who should have been supervising Parks and either didn't bother do their jobs, or placed far too much trust in him. LaDawn Stoddard, who managed the AmeriCorps program for the State of Utah, was aware of the issues in the auditor's report but apparently had decided that Parks could handle it all on his own. There were also questions about how well she knew the various rules, regulations and procedures governing the AmeriCorps program. Jared Steffy, who handled the money, relied on Parks' integrity, never bothering to verify or reconcile paperwork. Mike Gallegos, Parks' immediate supervisor, simply signed off on any documents Parks provided, maintaining only a "passive interest" in the operation, according to the auditor's report.

In short, Parks' higher–ups chose to leave it all in Parks' hands.

In February 2013, Parks pleaded guilty to two federal felonies. In September 2013 U.S. District Judge Robert Shelby waived prison time and sentenced him to 36 months probation and ordered him to pay $13,907 in restitution. In granting the lenient sentence, the Judge relied on the fact that Parks did not personally benefit and that he had no other interactions with the justice system.

Government auditing is essential in providing accountability to legislators, oversight bodies, those charged with governance, and the public. Audits provide an independent, objective, nonpartisan assessment of the stewardship, performance, or cost of government policies, programs, or operations, depending upon the type and scope of the audit.

— Comptroller General of the United States,
Government Auditing Standards 2011

CHAPTER 5

MIAMI-DADE COUNTY, FLORIDA, USA

The Jackson Health System includes a campus of six hospitals and health–care facilities that serve Miami–Dade County. Actually, "serve" might not be the right term here; the fabric of the well–being of the entire Miami–Dade Community is woven from Jackson Hospital cloth. In the words of the grand jury investigating it:

> Jackson Memorial Hospital (JMH) is our sainted jewel of an institution that we all rely on (even if we do not go there). For some, Jackson is the hospital that is there for those who have nowhere else to go. For others, it is the one we rely on when there is a medical problem that is beyond the ken of the average practitioner.

> We rely on Jackson. We need Jackson. Yet, those who had the responsibility of running this institution, as well as those who had the duty of oversight, have been irresponsible, complacent and reckless, and blindly relied on financial misstatements.

Corruption in Remission

From 2009 to 2011, Jackson lost a jaw–dropping $419 million—this against annual budgets of around $2 billion. Today, despite being yanked from the precipice in 2012, it still stands back only a few steps from the brink of insolvency, wiping its brow in relief. We're "one payroll away from not being liquid," according to board member Michael Bileca.

In the middle of 2011, after the $419 million was long gone and the hospital's survival had been put well and truly in question, an audit task force was finally called in to save the hospital. The auditors and a grand jury spent just under 60 days figuring out why Jackson was going broke.

After reading the audit report, Miami–Dade County handed the hospital's oversight to a career banker, Carlos Migoya, who put in place the audit team's eighteen recommendations. And after applying these strategies, Jackson stopped the $419 million hemorrhage and handed back a surplus of $18 million. This was the very next year, in 2012. When it turns around that fast, you know there was a lot of corruption.

Not everybody was happy. A union spokesperson, Martha Baker, complained about community praise for the new order. "This kumbaya stuff is very frustrating." And the new management system "is hardly a formula for long–term success," she groused.

What could be so controversial about a storybook ending like this one? Any time you bring order out of disorder, there is going to be weeping, wailing, and gnashing of teeth. At least this time, however, the weepers and wailers definitely did not include the patients who are cared for at Jackson.

Corruption Metastasized

The Hospital Governance Taskforce (HGT) auditors and the grand jury dug in and got to work to find the true causes of the mess. They reported that Jackson had been eaten alive by a financial three–headed hydra.

Head number one: A powerful union had extracted massive gains in salary and hiring levels, which resulted in labor costs that were far above health–care industry averages.

Head number two: The hospital had employed a long list of poor accounting methods, including failing to track accounts receivable, frequent billing failures, and badly implementing computer systems.

Head number three: A feud was ongoing between the health board that was supposed to manage the hospital, the Public Health Trust (PHT), and the Miami–Dade Board of County Commissioners (BCC). This conflict led to impotent management generally, and a particular lack of ability to act on budget problems.

The PHT was a body comprised of 17 members and was intended to keep effective day–to–day control over the hospital's service and efficiency. In reality, the PHT had come to be dominated by the politicians of the BCC. Of the 17 voting members, 16 had been either appointed by the BCC or were actual sitting commissioners.

Stage IV Labor Costs

The auditors and grand jury quickly learned about the One Big Secret to running a successful hospital. You have to control your labor costs. Ask any expert, go to anybody in the know, anybody who has ever been part of a well–run hospital, and you hear the same thing:

you can't pay salaries that are out of line with your budget. Control labor costs, and you've got a chance.

Successful hospitals, ones that run at a profit, maintain labor costs in the 40–41% range. Public hospitals may or may not survive if labor costs near 50%. But when auditors reviewed Jackson's financial statements, they found that JHS's labor costs had been 54–56% over the previous six years.

The PHT, which always understood how dire its checkbook woes were, tried desperately to negotiate a reasonable contract with the union. But when the PHT presented its streamlined budget proposal to the County for approval, the politicians of the BCC just overruled the PHT's decisions. They increased the union's wages, giving the union exactly the amount it asked for in the first place. Imagine the PHT's standing for future labor negotiations!

The BCC auditor—not the BCC board of politicians, but the auditors' office—tried to hold back the payroll tsunami that was washing Jackson away. The office sent letters, asking Jackson why its "Salaries and Related Costs" had zoomed 48% from 2002 to 2004, from $38 million to $56 million. However, an auditor can't help if he doesn't have any bite to go with his bark. Auditees are quick to understand when a letter can be ignored. Sometimes—as here—those audit fangs aren't granted until it's too late.

Meanwhile, the BCC and the PHT continued to point fingers back and forth. "Can we have a halfpenny surtax to fix things?" the PHT asked.

"How dare you ask for more money before you've gotten your own checkbook in order?" the BCC shot back. "Our voters don't like us raising taxes unless it's, you know, for something really important."

"But how can we get our checkbook in order when you overrule us every time we try to make a cut?" the PHT wailed.

The schizophrenia was easy to diagnose, but hospitals don't have much of an admissions process for unions or political boards.

Another example of the corruption culture: the PHT hired an outside firm, Deloitte, to teach it how to save money and operate efficiently. It paid $80M for some 200 binders' worth of information that would, the vendors said, teach PHT how to save $200M. Yet, the grand jury said, "as soon as Deloitte left we were told that things at JMH reverted back to 'business as usual.' Many witnesses referred to this as the longstanding "culture at Jackson.'"

So, the PHT not only dropped the ball on the $200M in savings, but it also squandered the $80M spent to learn how to save the $200M. There seemed no way to overcome the inertia and confusion at Jackson.

Cut, Burn, Poison

The auditors and grand jury were clear about the steps needed to eliminate the corruption.

"Put this hospital in the hands of people who are not going to kowtow to the BCC," they said, "and put it into the hands of people who are not beholden to the unions." And do it yesterday.

The auditors' and grand jury members' instructions were to:

1. Define a mission statement that captures the new culture that was needed.
2. Appoint a diverse and expert nine–member board, with five of them appointed by the Mayor rather than by the BCC.
3. Set a conflict–of–interest policy and give it fangs down to its chin—for example, prohibit the board from hiring contractors that employ family members.
4. Get the legislative changes to Miami–Dade County

ordinances that will give real autonomy to the new Jackson oversight board.

5. Appoint a Public Health Advisory Committee—essentially a permanent audit team—to make sure that public funds are being spent as intended.
6. Ensure that Jackson remains eligible for important sources of public funding.

And so on until there were 18 specific recommendations.

Career banker Carlos Migoya took over and changed the culture fast. He identified the unnecessary labor and after he made the first real cuts, he had people's attention. Union reps closed their mouths so fast you could hear their teeth click, and the culture changed. In less than a year, 920 entitlement workers had been laid off. Process inefficiencies were laid off even faster.

These weren't just mindless cuts by Migoya. He added back almost 350 part–time employees, creating a flexible work force that could adjust to varying patient volumes.

Migoya saw to it that the JMH Health Plan was restructured; this alone went from a $26 million yearly deficit to an $18 million surplus. Many other tough but sensible business decisions followed. And the jewel that they rely on today stands ready to care for Miami–Dade people for decades to come.

We cannot don the role of cheerleaders. We strive to provide objective feedback on the functioning of the various departments of the government. The time has come when we will all be held responsible for our actions, the way the foundations of an ideal society are laid. One cannot compromise with integrity, whether in public administration or corporate administration.

—Vinod Rai, Comptroller and Auditor General of India (2008–2013)

CHAPTER 6

COAL INDUSTRY, INDIA

In 2008, Vinod Rai was ready to retire from a dutiful career as an accountant in India's Ministry of Finance when his life took an unexpected turn. To everyone's surprise, Rai was asked to accept a one–time, six–year position as the Comptroller and Auditor General (CAG) for his country. During his tenure, this genial auditor worked tirelessly and fearlessly in his new and demanding role.

It is highly doubtful that anyone expected such an unassuming numbers–cruncher to spearhead a powerful charge against government corruption and graft at the highest levels of his country. However, during his tenure, Rai has made the Office of the CAG a potent force for accountability and transparency in modern India.

The Office of the CAG is highly regarded in India and sits on par with the Supreme Court. Its integrity is guarded by term limits and restrictions against securing future government positions. The holder of this position can be removed only by impeachment. While the Office of the Auditor sends reports directly to Parliament, it is not required to answer to India's governing body. The CAG presides over more than 63,000 employees. Rai's first decision in his new position was to avoid wasting time and resources on endless rounds of nit–picking, and instead to concentrate the efforts of his office where the risk of misgovernment was the greatest. One such area that demanded immediate attention would eventually become known as "Coalgate."

Whose Dirty Hands Are Covered with Coal?

As a predominantly socialist country, India controlled and directed large sectors of its economy through Five–Year Plans. In 1973, the government passed the Coal Mines Nationalisation Act, which basically captured coal–mining land for public–sector needs. It also divided the majority of available territory into land grants, or "coal blocks" and then parceled most of them out to the two state–owned companies: Coal India Limited (CIL) and Singareni Collieries Company Ltd. (SCCL). Each coal block was intended to address a specific energy need in the country. In 1976, the Nationalisation Act was amended to terminate all private coal–mining leases except for those of companies that were producing iron and steel or operating in extremely isolated areas.

In 1992, the Ministry of Coal created a Screening Committee whose job was to determine which private companies would be awarded the additional 143 land blocks not already allocated to CIL and SCCL. An additional 1993 amendment added private companies that were supporting power generation and cement production to the eligibility list. Qualifying businesses could now be granted coal blocks for no more than the price of the original geological report for each piece of land, a mere pittance compared to the value of working the property.

During the years from 1993–2005, the Screening Committee, lacking any clear policy, handed out coal blocks on as little as a single letter of recommendation, a procedure that was ripe for favoritism, bribery, and corruption. In 2005, in an attempt to address this problematic issue, a government–appointed expert committee presented Coal Sector Reforms that were designed to make the allocation of coal blocks more transparent and fair. It recommended that the government work in conjunction with CIL and SCCL to identify blocks for allocation. They would then advertise available coal–mining land in India's national newspapers and parcel out only a few pieces at a time. Still, there were no specific criteria for applicants beyond preferring those associated with power, steel, iron, and cement. Occasionally, financial history and net worth were considered, but in many cases, it appeared that personal favoritism played a huge part in the decision–making process.

Between 2004 and 2009, an incredible 44 billion metric tons of coal were allocated to public and private companies. For the price of a geology report, these businesses were able to hoard hundreds of years' worth of this valuable fossil fuel. In 2010, the government passed a bill requiring that coal blocks be sold through a process of competitive bidding, thus putting an end to the massive coal give–away of the previous years.

Someone Leaks the Bad News

In March 2012, the rough draft of the CAG's report, "Performance Audit of the Allocation of Coal Blocks and Augmentation of Coal Production by Coal India Limited," was leaked to the press. Its scope was the 11th Five–Year Plan covering the years 2007 to 2012. However, the review looked at coal–block allocations dating back to 2004. The Auditor's office examined the financial records of the

Ministry of Coal, the Coal Controller's Organisation, Coal India Ltd., and its subsidiaries. They studied any policies, guidelines and procedures that addressed the allocation of coal blocks, the monitoring of coal production, the distribution of coal and its pricing. Findings were held up to the mirror of the Planning Commission's original coal–production projections and the performance parameters of the Ministry of Coal and CIL. All agencies cooperated with the investigation. This particular audit was aimed primarily at CIL, and its findings were not pretty:

- CIL had been given an 81 percent monopoly on coal production.
- CIL had not kept up with expected production quotas, despite new projects and outsourcing efforts.
- Because of the lack of coal, critical capacities in the power sector were forced to sit idle or limited in their ability to function.
- The gap between the demand for coal and CIL's ability to provide was ever widening.
- Other allocated coal blocks were failing to produce significantly.
- The process that allocated coal blocks was highly suspect.

For those in power, the findings of the CAG were awkward, to say the least. The government was accused of gross inefficiency in allocating coal blocks during the period 2004–2009. Although it had the jurisdiction and authority to switch to competitive bidding in 2004, the governing bodies chose to continue to award coal blocks solely based on what appeared to be personal interests. As a result, Public Sector Enterprises (PSEs) and 100 private coal–mining companies paid far less than they should have for their coal block grants. The draft audit estimated their combined windfall gains at US$ 201.72 billion. The final audit would slash that number to US$

35.08 billion, but that was still the equivalent of decades of coal needs for the country of India.

Although the CAG Performance Audit never expressly charged the government with corruption, it was a small step for the media and the general public to take. *The Times* of India quickly dubbed the coal scandal "The Mother of All Scams."

THE FALLOUT

Often, corruption seeks to protect itself. The response was fast and furious.

Prime Minister Manmohan Singh offered to "retire from public life" if this report proved true. When it did prove to be true, he simply read a statement rebutting the report in terms of its understanding of the law and its estimated cost to the Indian public. He remained in office until his party was defeated in 2014.

Government officials called the report a "piece of trash" and tried to discredit Vinod Rai and the office of the CAG.

The Supreme Court of India was called in to rule on the legitimacy of the CAG. Because the office is actually included in the Constitution of India and given "ninth stature," the same as of the Supreme Court, you can imagine how that turned out. The CAG was upheld as a "constitutional authority."

The opposition, the Bharatiya Janata Party (BJP), was delighted to charge the government with corruption, and filed a complaint with the Central Vigilance Committee requesting a court–monitored probe. The Central Vigilance Committee directed the Central Bureau of Intelligence to conduct a thorough investigation. Suspicions of bribery and cronyism resulted in personal investigations of many influential government figures.

Twelve firms were charged with overstating their net worth to improve their chances for receiving allocations, failing to disclose prior coal land grants, and hoarding rather than developing their coal blocks.

The BJP demanded that Prime Minister Singh resign. He refused. Feelings ran so high that Parliament was actually only able to work together for seven of the 20 days immediately following the revelation of the scandal.

And Mr. Rai received death threats.

Moving Forward

During the heavy–duty fallout from his performance audit and the personal attacks on his character, Vinod Rai maintained his calm demeanor. He firmly maintained his position that, "One cannot compromise with integrity whether in public administration or in corporate administration." Unintentionally, he had helped the CAG to become "a source of hope at a time of growing despair over India's rotten governance." Other political bombshells have rocked the country since the Coalgate Scandal, but Vinod Rai continued to stand confidently, determined to call forth the best in the country he loves, even if that means exposing the worst for all to see.

He gazed for what seemed an age, before drawn almost against his will, he stole from the shadow of the doorway, across the floor to the nearest edge of the mounds of treasure. Above him the sleeping dragon lay, a dire menace even in his sleep. He grasped a great two-handled cup, as heavy as he could carry, and cast one fearful eye upwards. Smaug stirred a wing, opened a claw, the rumble of his snoring changed its note.
Then Bilbo fled.

— J.R.R. Tolkien, *The Hobbit*

CHAPTER 7

SISKIYOU COUNTY, CALIFORNIA, USA

For some auditors, a perfect world would be one in which every investigation nabs a real crook and every dollar is returned to its rightful owner. But other auditors float their boats on a river that is a much brighter blue than that—in their perfect world, not a single dollar is ever taken in the first place.

A good audit recovers funds. A great audit recovers funds, and scares the pants off thieves who might have been contemplating their sordid gain through similar channels. But an excellent audit can prevent loss before it ever occurs.

That should have been the way in 2012, when advance inspections could have prevented the theft of millions of dollars in gold from the Siskiyou County Courthouse in Yreka, California.

The Best Smash-and-Grab in Town

On February 1, 2012, two young men broke into the County Courthouse at 1 a.m. and used a crowbar to smash a lobby display case. A pretty straightforward smash–and–grab, right? What did they make off with, a case of beer?

No, in the courthouse there sat a display that held $3 million worth of historical gold that had been mined in the area. The collection served as the spiritual maypole around which the whole community danced. Yreka owes its existence to the 1851 gold rush. To this day its primary income revolves around tourism that celebrates the gold mining of long ago.

It didn't exactly take the Pink Panther to plan the heist. Surveillance video was posted all over the internet, and it showed that the thieves leisurely wandered in and helped themselves to the millions in gold. The robbers showed all the style and élan of sedated zombies, shuffling in, busting open the case, and shuffling out slowly and stiffly with seven figures' worth of pure gold.

In hindsight, you wonder why thieves from all over the globe weren't holding fistfights in the parking lot to pull the job. What was a museum–quality collection doing in an old historical building with minimal security? Why were the property managers okay with the risk?

Why, for that matter, hadn't the financially–challenged little town ever sold that much gold in order to balance its budget?

How Ironic—You Can't Buy Gold in Yreka

In 2010, county officials received several attractive offers for their collection. They decided against selling their gold hoard. As Claudia East, vice president of the Siskiyou County Historical Society once put it, "Living here, especially in Yreka, is like living in a Norman Rockwell painting." People sit on their front porches and chat, and "if a kid comes down the sidewalk on a skateboard, he'll stop and get off to let you pass before getting back on." The sheriff of Mayberry probably would have given you the same chuckle if you'd tried to buy his police cruiser. Thanks, amigo, but we do things a little differently around these parts.

Yreka boomed when a mule train packer, Abraham Thompson, found gold there in 1851. Quickly the area was flooded with tinpanners and miners, and the city became known as the richest square mile in California. The little town became known as "the second Mother Lode," after San Francisco.

Nowadays the gold is mined out, and the logging and mineral industries are also played out. But the school colors are still red and gold, the sports mascot is a gold miner, and so forth. The townspeople still have their heritage, and they have the tourism that goes with it.

The town's name itself, Yreka, seems to be taken from a Mark Twain palindrome, Yreka Bakery. Maybe somebody had a Bakery sign up, the B fell off, and somebody else read the sign from the rear side? The point is, tourists come through often enough to keep the town going.

Buy your old–timey gold hoard, sirs? We don't suppose you'd ask a Philadelphia councilman to sell the Liberty Bell to balance the 2012 budget.

We admire Yreka's honor and integrity. But keep in mind what this also means: Yreka's gold collection was worth far *more* than the $3 million the city turned down. It was worth $3 million to anybody. What was it worth to the town, then?

Not Exactly Fort Knox

Okay, the museum gold stays. We get it. But what about the security? The thieves who made off with the gold had to figure out how to get in a bathroom window. Boom, they had all the time they wanted in the unattended lobby. Once they were in, they could have used dynamite if they'd wanted.

Security apparently consisted of a panel of "indestructible" glass, a silent alarm on the case, and a video camera. Avoid that and all you have to do is drive home safely.

A museum security consulting firm would probably be aghast. For starters, museum security standards hold that nobody should be able to approach the perimeter of a building that holds a valuable painting, much less get inside with little trouble and nobody watching. Fences and gates that are tough to defeat should keep robbers a good distance away from the *outside* walls. Contrast that with the quaint old Siskiyou County Courthouse, a quilt of structures some parts of which are 150 years old.

If you want to send a security chief screaming into the night, mention to him that the gold display, and the rickety old courthouse, were featured statewide on TV in a 2007 episode of "California's Gold." No word on whether a neon sign was installed on top of the building, blinking HUGE GOLD CACHE SITTING DIRECTLY BELOW THIS ARROW.

A security firm will narrow its eyes—rightly—and glare suspiciously at every single door and window as a potential entry point. That same firm will assume that in the coming year, expert robbers from everywhere on earth will target the hoard for termination. You think it's worth a plane ticket from anywhere in the world to visit a 150–year–old building with a $3 million stash of gold?

Here again, contrast the unsecured bathroom window that allowed the thieves access. It is first principles for a museum to have early–warning glass break detection on every window—that's assuming even that the display room absolutely must have windows in it.

Museum standards also insist on vibration sensors for the display, motion–detection devices that bathe the entire room, and so forth. With $3 million in gold on display, they might at the very least have had a volunteer(ish) security guard, and/or a local city official's pooch, one with good–sized fangs, roaming the halls at night.

A (Troy) Ounce of Prevention

You might have wondered when we were getting to the auditor in this case. The takeaway here is a simple one: audits before the fact are better than audits after the fact. It is any auditor's job to reduce risk and to point out where potential loss, or waste, exists. An ounce of prevention is worth quite a few pounds of gold, as it were.

An auditor might easily have called a museum–class consultant for a special security audit. For a few hundred or perhaps a few thousand dollars, a consulting firm could have provided a report to the Yreka council.

Or perhaps they did? If so, the blame is on the council for giving insufficient weight to the recommendations. Now they'd love to pay a $50,000 reward for information leading to ... well, you know the rest.

My business in this state
Made me a looker on here in Vienna,
Where I have seen corruption boil and bubble
Till it o'er-run the stew; laws for all faults,
But faults so countenanced, that the strong statutes
Stand like the forfeits in a barber's shop,
As much in mock as mark.

—William Shakespeare, *Measure for Measure*, V.i

CHAPTER 8

ORANGE COUNTY, CALIFORNIA, USA

Carlos Bustamante was an executive with the Public Works Department of Orange County, as well as a Santa Ana city councilman. Bustamante began working for Orange County in 2000. A favored Latino in the Republican party, Bustamante was awarded promotions and raises until, by 2011, his salary was $178,277 for his position as the Director of Administrative Services at the Public Works Department. Some found his increasing salary questionable, but that had nothing to do with his sudden resignation in October 2011.

More than a dozen women alleged that over eight years they endured sexually charged attacks in stairwells and elevators, and behind locked office doors. The Human Resources Department of the county received several complaints of sexual harassment by Bustamante but did nothing. Frustrated employees began to release letters to the news media and the Internal Audit Hotline. One anonymous letter to the county Internal Audit Hotline, which detailed walking into a conference room and unexpectedly observing him in the act of having sex with a female employee, motivated some action. Why did it take so long for Bustamante to be stopped?

Auditing an Investigation

Dr. Peter Hughes has served as the Director of Internal Audit for Orange County since his appointment in 1999 by the Orange County Board of Supervisors. He has both the knowledge and the experience for this kind of work. Hughes' assignment was to examine whether the HR Department handled a specific sexual harassment case in accordance with federal and procedures and to determine if the county was at risk for litigation.

Peter Hughes' investigation blew the doors wide open. Although stone–walled for months by the HR Department, he investigated allegations received through the Internal Audit Hotline in three separate letters, an independent internal report, two meetings with the HR staff of Public Works, and other HR Department responses. The evidence showed a pattern of feigned ignorance, cover–ups and pass–the–buck management.

Almost every witness who spoke with Hughes expressed real fear of backlash for participating in the investigation. Instead of viewing the HR Department as a valuable, supportive resource, employees consistently voiced grave concern that they would experience retaliation for providing information. Two employees adamantly refused to speak in the presence of any member of HR staff. Witnesses had absolutely no confidence that HR officers, if left to themselves, would conduct any sort of legitimate investigation into these very serious complaints.

Peter Hughes' eye–opening report was completed on February 29, 2012 and delivered to the Orange County Board of Supervisors shortly thereafter. It found that the Public Works HR Department had taken a position of deliberate inaction when presented with sexual harassment complaints filed by female employees.

Not only did Hughes' report fault the Human Resources Department, but it laid blame on other shoulders as well, including Public Works Director Jess Carbajal, who was Bustamante's direct supervisor. He had received a detailed formal complaint containing two allegations about Bustamante's behavior with female employees in March 2011. Although he shared this information with County CEO Tom Mauk and Board of Supervisors Chairman Bill Campbell, he violated EEO policy by not bringing the allegations to the HR Department. As a result, the HR Department claimed it was not aware of the problem until it launched its own investigation in response to complaints received through the Internal Audit Hotline. Carbajal, Mauk, and Campbell also chose to withhold this information from the Board of Supervisors, County Counsel, and the Internal Auditors.

The Auditor's four–page report outlined glaring shortcomings in the County's handling of the allegations against Bustamante. It dealt with the issues of who knew what, when they knew it, and what they did or did not do about it. As with any good audit, it also offered valuable recommendations for the future:

- The County's harassment policy should be reviewed and updated.
- The County's harassment policy should require all allegations to be promptly investigated.
- Complaints should be kept as confidential as possible to avoid retaliation.
- Promotions should be based solely on who is better qualified.
- Measures should be enacted to encourage collaborative reporting.

Hughes' report confirmed what County Counsel Nicholas S. Chrisos feared: Orange County was now vulnerable to sexual harassment liability claims.

Ultimately, the audit report prompted District Attorney Tony Rackauckas to start a criminal investigation. Carlos Bustamante was arrested on July 2, 2012 and charged with 12 felonies and four misdemeanors, some of which dated as far back as 2003 and involved at least seven women who were willing to come forward when they finally knew they had a voice. Charges included false imprisonment, sexual battery, stalking, and theft. Public Works director Jess Carbajal was fired "with cause" a week later. Carbajal's direct supervisor, Orange County Deputy CEO Alisa Drakodaidis immediately took medical leave. CEO Tom Mauk resigned under pressure the following month. Thanks to the objective evidence gathered by Peter Hughes and the Office of Internal Audit, Public Works' dirty little secret was exposed. Now at last, justice could be served.

Legal Moralism and Lawyer Narrowing

Sexual harassment encompasses a broad spectrum of reprehensible behaviors. It is also corrupt in the sense that it hinders an organization from accomplishing its purposes. Sexual harassment is considered a form of discrimination that violates the United States' Civil Rights Act of 1964. An employee who violates the rules can face severe consequences including job loss, demotion, or even prison.

The Equal Employment Opportunity Commission (EEOC) has codified those behaviors that constitute sexual harassment and has designed detailed management and employee training materials on the subject. However, codifying ethical rules often results in more, not less, bad behavior. When ethical rules are codified, there is an implication that anything that isn't specifically prohibited is allowable. Individuals are relieved from applying their own moral principles to the situation, and some engage in conduct that is close to the margins of the law, but well outside appropriate workplace conduct. This is called legal moralism.

This effect is exacerbated when those accused of inappropriate conduct hire lawyers to defend them. A lawyer presented with a fact situation and a code provision will develop an argument that the conduct is not included in the rule. Over time, lawyers narrow the application of written rules. When it comes to codifying sexual harassment rules, legal moralism and lawyers narrowing the application results in some people becoming less likely to keep behavior within acceptable boundaries. It is reasonable to expect that codification may actually increase sexual harassment.

In fact, sexual harassment in the workplace appears to be growing rather than shrinking. In 2012, the EEOC received more than 15,000 employee complaints of this nature, up from 11,717 cases in 2010. These figures do not include the frustrated employees who sought private help through their own lawyers or chose to handle their situations in some other manner. Codification of ethical rules is not the only tool for addressing sexual harassment. In fact, addressing sexual harassment as corruption without initially focusing on culpability can yield better results.

Sexual Harassment is a Form of Corruption

Female employees make the vast majority of sexual harassment complaints. It is estimated that 40 to 70 percent of all women can expect to be sexually harassed at their place of employment. According to the EEOC, 62 percent of these victims will not complain because they do not believe that justice will be served and they fear the threat of retaliation and backlash for simply reporting culpable conduct. Instead, half of them will try to tolerate the abuse, 24 percent will start taking extra time off because of the additional stress, 10 percent will walk away from their job, and all will suffer loss in work satisfaction and productivity.

It isn't just victims that are negatively affected by sexual harassment. An organization that overlooks such offensive behavior suffers in decreased employee morale, increased absenteeism, loss of production, and possible costly litigation settlements. In 2010, American businesses paid out more than $48 million in monetary benefits for this problem, not including additional monies paid through litigation procedures. From both the company's and the victim's position, sexual harassment is a "lose–lose" situation. It is corruption, plain and simple.

But sexual harassment is usually not addressed as corruption. Usually, the tactics employed focus on the culpable conduct. Sexual harassment often involves acts that are intentional, offensive, disrespectful, and worthy of blame. However, people willing to point the finger of blame at their enemies can abuse the procedures that are used to catch and punish bad actors. Thus, one type of corruption—sexual harassment—is exchanged for two more—investigations that are disruptive and investigations that lead to inaccurate results.

The consequences to the harasser, even for a minor or technical violation, can be catastrophic. The organization is also disrupted by sexual harassment investigations and punishments. The consequences can be so significant that the people who administer the procedure do not have the stomach to administer the consequences. They will not act to destroy someone's life. The tension between culpable conduct, procedures that can be manipulated, and severe consequences lead to a system that is complicated, does not always lead to the correct result, and does not eliminate the corruption it is intended to address.

In the end, it isn't structure and processes that eliminate corruption. It is individual people who do the right thing, whether it's people who don't sexually harass others, or managers who don't cover it up, or auditors who uncover it.

‘cor·rupt verb \kə’rəpt
transitive verb
1 a : to change from good to bad in morals, manners, or actions; also : bribe
b : to degrade with unsound principles or moral values
. . .
4 : to alter from the original or correct form or version <the file was corrupted>

— Merriam–Webster Dictionary

CHAPTER 9

WINDCREST, TEXAS, USA

Stealing is never justified. However, there are some situations in which one could perhaps empathize with the perpetrator. Life is economically difficult for many people in today’s economy. Some people struggle with paying their rent or mortgage. Some people have difficulty feeding their families. Some people are mentally ill. Some people have issues with addictions, whether chemical or otherwise, and are unable to get the treatment they need.

But some people have it all. They have plenty of money, a secure job, respect in the community. Yet they want more and more. They feel entitled to it, and when they’re caught with their hands in the proverbial cookie jar, they continue to insist they did nothing wrong.

According to a report issued by the security firm Marquet

International, the primary motive for embezzlement is sheer, simple greed. And while women are more likely to embezzle than men when the opportunity arises, men tend to steal larger amounts—*much* larger amounts.

The Cains Are Able

Most real estate developers make a very nice living, and 54–year–old Gary Cain of Windcrest, Texas, was no exception. In 2006, Gary saw an excellent opportunity as the San Antonio suburb was looking to attract new industry in the form of Rackspace U.S. Inc., a major web–hosting firm. There was only one problem: the abandoned mall property Rackspace was considering consisted of four separate pieces. It was necessary to consolidate these into a single property and renovate the run–down structures. This in turn required the assistance of a developer who was able to raise funds for the acquisition of all the sections, then turn around and sell the consolidated property to Rackspace. In exchange for this service, the developer would take a "small" profit as a fee. "Small" in this case could be in the six–figure range, not bad for a single transaction. "Project Castle," as the project was called, would eventually bring 4500 full–time jobs to the community.

There were likely a number of developers who would have liked to get in on this deal. However, Gary Cain had an inside track: it so happened that his older brother, Ronnie, was the City Manager, a post he had held for over a quarter–century. Prior to that, he had been the Windcrest Chief of Police. Ronnie Cain was a solid member of the community upon whom citizens had relied for years.

This raises the question of a conflict of interest, but in Windcrest, this apparently wasn't a problem. Nepotism may be unethical, but as long as Ronnie had no financial interests or other connections to his brother's real estate development company, there was nothing illegal about it.

Eventually, three entities formed a partnership for the purpose of realizing Project Castle. These were:

- Rackspace US, Inc.
- Windcrest Economic Development Corporation (WWEDC)
- Windcrest Economic Development Company, LLC (WEDC)

WWEDC was a business entity legally separate from the city, but considered a department of the municipal government. It was accountable to the City Manager, Ronnie Cain, and ultimately the City Council. WEDC, with its remarkably similar name, was a firm established by Gary Cain for the purpose of raising funds for the project.

It was not coincidental that Gary chose that particular name—and it wasn't the only company involved with Project Castle that had been given a name very similar to that of another well–established company participating in the project.

All in the Family

In early 2007, shortly after Rackspace decided upon the old Windsor Mall location, Ronnie Cain charged the city's Financial Officer, Betsy Mills, with the task of opening a bank account for the project in the name of "City of Windcrest—Project Castle." The money in this account would be used to cover the developer's (Gary Cain's) costs and account for them in one place. Gary was supposed to fund the account. The opening deposit was a check for $68,000. Oddly, Ronnie Cain signed the check.

Later, Mills told law enforcement that she and other city employees received instructions from the city auditor that they "should not continue to handle a bank account funded by Gary Cain in order to avoid potential problems." At the end of May 2007, Ronnie Cain ordered Mills to hand over the checkbook, bank statements, and other documents related to the Project Castle account, informing her that all future transactions would be "handled by the investment group" rather than the city.

Six months later, Ronnie wrote a check on the Project Castle account that was used to open an account at another bank in the name of "Urban Revitalization Real Estate Group—Project Castle." Over the next twenty–two months, around $340,000 was deposited in this account. The money came not from Gary Cain, but either from the City of Windcrest itself or from one of the other accounts maintained by the municipal government. At the same time, Ronnie Cain wrote a number of small checks ($200–$400) to the City of Windcrest and then, according to Mills, he would remove the corresponding amount of money from the cash drawer.

Although the "Urban" account (as it was later identified by a law enforcement officer) was meant to keep track of and cover development expenses connected to Project Castle, Ronnie Cain took out $70,000 for his own personal use. $20,000 of it wound up in the personal account of the Windcrest City Secretary, an attractive woman named Tracy Freimarck. (And the answer is yes, he was.)

Finally, in July 2007, Gary Cain received a $300,000 loan from the city. Paula Miles, who was President of the WWEDC (the corporation controlled by the City of Windcrest), said it was a surprise to her. Neither she nor the WWEDC Board of directors was aware that Gary Cain had even asked for the loan. In any event, any loan or grant of that size made to a local business would have required the approval of the board.

Gary Cain was ambitious. He saw not only a new headquarters for a rapidly growing Internet company, but he also envisioned multi– and single–family housing units, retail stores, offices, restaurants, and entertainment venues in the surrounding area.

Between the Rackspace jobs and jobs created through development, Project Castle promised to be a boon for the entire community.

Rackspace US, Inc. signed on the dotted line at the beginning of August 2007. The agreement outlined Rackspace's obligations in return for economic incentives, including tax abatement, provided by the city. Under the terms of the agreement, Gary Cain's company (WEDC) would fund the city's purchase of the mall property. The city would then sell the property to Rackspace for the actual purchase price, plus any fees involved. The agreement also required Rackspace to deposit $5 million into an escrow account in order to pay for development expenses, specifically, those incurred with land located south of the mall, known as the "Eisenhauer Development Tract."

Sworn affidavits signed by Gary Cain and presented to both the city and Rackspace stated that the total purchase price of the properties was just under $27 million. According to local investigative reporter John Tedesco, the purpose of these affidavits was to "prove that Rackspace's lease did not exceed the cost of acquiring the properties." The affidavits also stated that Gary's brother, Ronnie, was fully aware of the land's fair market value, and Ronnie had nothing to add at the meeting in which Gary presented the affidavits to the city and Rackspace representatives.

Here's where it gets interesting. Under the terms of the agreement Rackspace had signed with the City as well as Gary Cain's WEDC, Rackspace was entitled to a Certification of Costs from the other parties, if for no other reason than to make certain the purchase price was in line with the fair market value of the land. Prior to signing the agreement, Rackspace representatives had repeatedly requested a Certification of Costs that supported Gary Cain's figures. Gary Cain replied that he was under a confidentiality agreement with the seller, and Rackspace and the City would simply have to take his word for it. After all, he had provided sworn affidavits, and his brother, the City

Manager, didn't say anything different.

The following March, a company known as "DDPZ," which had offices in Miami as well as Texas, presented the City of Windcrest with a bill for $2.8 million. Significantly, one of the companies involved in Project Castle, hired to improve vehicle access to the new Rackspace facility, was Duany Plater–Zyberk and Company, a prominent, well–respected architectural firm founded by a husband–wife team in 1980, which had an office at the same Miami address. The invoice received by the city was on official letterhead and was carefully worded. For all intents and purposes, it looked legitimate. Nobody asked questions when City Manager Ronnie Cain transferred $2.8 million out of the Project Castle escrow account to the city's general account, then presented the invoice to Mayor Jack Leonhardt, who approved the payment, even though no actual work on the access road had been done. DDPZ received its payment on 11 April 2008.

Andres Duany, who operates Duany Plater–Zyberk and Company with his wife Elizabeth Plater–Zyberk, was a bit mystified when he was contacted about the payment, which he had not received, for work that had barely been started. He was also disturbed by the unauthorized use of his Miami business address by a company with a name similar to that of his own, but that was definitely *not* his firm. Duany's concern triggered some inquiries, which revealed that the local address associated DDPZ bank account was a UPS store and that one of the signers on the account was Gary Cain. When investigators dug a little deeper, they discovered that the account had been opened with a check for $100,000 drawn on Ronnie's "Urban" account about two weeks before Ronnie Cain had presented the city with an invoice from "DDPZ".

Another address was listed as well: a condominium that Gary had purchased at the end of May, then signed over to a Cain company called "Lyn Family III, LP."

The noose was tightening, but the Cain brothers were blissfully unaware that their days of living high on the hog were numbered. For the next year, Gary Cain spent like a rap star, buying expensive jewelry and furniture, treating himself to holidays in New York, Los Angeles and Puerto Rico, and throwing a lavish party for his beloved daughter on the occasion of her sixteenth birthday. The shindig included a hip hop concert as well as gifts such as designer shoes and a brand new luxury SUV, courtesy of Jaguar Motors, Ltd. The celebration was so over–the–top that it attracted the attention of producers at MTV and was featured on the network's reality show, *My Super Sweet Sixteen.*

At the same time, Ronnie failed to inform his brother's business partners that he had authorized the $2.8 million payment to DDPZ. In fact, he informed the partners that the escrow account still contained not only the original $5 million, but an extra $132,000 on top of it! An audit of the account came to a much different conclusion.

Am I My Brother's Co-Defendant?

By February 2009, work on the access road had not progressed, and over half of the funds allocated for that part of Project Castle had already been paid out. The people at Rackspace were understandably upset that the money had been spent with almost nothing to show for it. Gary Cain was going to have hard questions to answer.

And answer them he did, by threatening to drag the city into impending litigation with Rackspace! He also threatened to use his position to block further development south of the mall. The board of WWEDC (the city entity) was so intimidated, it recommended that Gary be paid off (to the tune of $300,000) in order to make him go away.

By the end of the summer, the City Council was on the verge of settling with Gary Cain.

The music stopped in August 2009. Rackspace had discovered,

through an examination of the original property deeds, that Gary Cain's WEDC had padded the price of the property by almost $7 million, nearly a third more than the land had been worth. Then, there was the matter of the $2.8 million missing from the Project Castle escrow account. Rackspace filed a lawsuit in an attempt to recover their money, in addition to having been sold a parcel of land it was beginning to look as if the company would never be able to use. The company also filed suit against Cain's business partners, one of whom had paid out half a million to Andres Duany's company in good faith and for which he had never been reimbursed. Those partners filed suit against both Cain brothers the following June.

As the litigation storm gathered momentum, Ronnie Cain decided it was time to cut his losses and jump ship. He resigned his position as City Manager, a job he had held for twenty–eight years, in May 2010. At the time, he insisted it had nothing to do with any sort of impropriety, or the investigation that had been started by the Texas Rangers (the law enforcement agency).

In November, the City of Windcrest filed a civil lawsuit against its former City Manager. That same month, the criminal justice system got involved as charges of embezzlement and money laundering were filed against both Cain brothers. Less than a month later, the City intervened in the Rackspace lawsuit, pursuing its own civil case against Gary Cain and his business partners. The partners in turn filed a cross–claim against Windcrest, claiming the city had committed fraud when they persuaded them to participate in Project Castle. At almost the same time, Gary Cain, who experienced "chest pains" as he was being taken into custody by law enforcement and blamed the alleged "heart condition" on the stress caused by the experience, filed a defamation suit against the City of Windcrest for $400 million.

The icing on this litigious cake came in May 2011, when Ronnie Cain sued his former employer for severance pay, even though he had resigned of his own volition.

Between the civil litigation and the criminal prosecution (which has been postponed multiple times), lawyers, judges, and jury members will be kept busy for a very long time.

In addition to his duties as an investigative reporter for the *San Antonio Express News,* John Tedesco publishes a blog on his own website. He was able to dig up some old dirt on Gary Cain of which the city council should have been aware prior to doing business with him. He writes:

> Two years before the Rackspace deal, two banks each sued Gary Cain and his partners for bank fraud over loans used to buy some small Louisiana hospitals . . . [and] misrepresenting the value of collateral for the loans. . . . in Bexar County, the IRS in early 2007 filed federal tax liens totaling $1.4 million against another of Cain's companies connected with the hospitals.

Quoting a CPA who has investigated several cases of public fraud, Tedesco also writes, "a background check of Gary Cain by Windcrest should have been 'a routine thing considering the relationships.'"

There was also much left to be desired with the city's system of internal controls, which an auditor working with a San Francisco consulting firm described as a "gooey mess."

Then, there is the issue of trust and old, established relationships with neighbors and colleagues. One city council member told Tedesco that she had worked with Ronnie Cane for over two decades. "I trusted him," she said, adding, "He seemed to have done a good job . . . if any of the allegations are true, I feel betrayed personally and for the community."

As of October 2012, the Cain brothers were still asserting their innocence. During his lawsuit against the City of Windcrest, Gary Cain found himself in a difficult situation during the deposition. The judge in the case told him if he insisted on exercising his Fifth Amendment rights, he would lose his cause of action, but in order to pursue his civil case against the city, he would have to provide potentially self–incriminating answers to the defense lawyer's inquiries.

He chose to drop the case. He could potentially refile the lawsuit if found not guilty in the still–pending criminal trial, however. As of this writing, his wife is divorcing him, and both he and his brother have filed for bankruptcy. The City of Windcrest is also attempting to seize the brothers' condominium, valued at around $274,000, a small fraction of the community's total financial losses.

During the summer of 2012, the City of Windcrest was able to sell off the Windsor Park mall property, thus relieving itself of further obligations and liabilities. However, the taxpayers still lost several million dollars because of the Cain brother's corruption. This loss is not only due to the Cain brothers' alleged theft, but also years of property taxes that weren't collected while the Project Castle agreement was in force. In addition, there was a bank note for $17 million, for which the city had put up the land as collateral. The land was sold to a party who can proceed with development, and hopefully one day, the citizens of Windcrest will see some benefit from it.

We hold these truths to be self-evident, that all men are created equal, that they are endowed by their Creator with certain unalienable Rights, that among these are Life, Liberty and the pursuit of Happiness—That to secure these rights, Governments are instituted among Men, deriving their just powers from the consent of the governed,— . . .

— The Declaration of Independence

CHAPTER 10
WASHINGTON, DC, USA

In several parts of the country, 1999 was a pivotal year in the tenuous relationship between the public and the police force. The World Trade Organization in Seattle attracted anti–globalization groups and anarchists who were both organized and violent. They deliberately trashed property and attacked police officers with an ugly vengeance. In response, local peacekeepers pulled out the tear gas and pepper spray, imposed curfews, and arrested almost 500 attendees. However, rather than appearing grateful, the citizens of Seattle seemed more shocked and offended at the heavy–handed police response than they were at the problems caused by the protestors.

Just two short years later in 2001, the threat of terrorism on American soil became a haunting reality. Americans learned to expect reports of evil of apocalyptic proportions with their daily morning coffee. Overnight, a boatload of anti–terrorism laws, policies, and procedures opened wide the door for unlawful police activity under the guise of emergency measures to protect a nation under attack. Since that time, ferreting out any and every potential foreign threat has become the top priority for law enforcement in major cities across this country—and perhaps nowhere more so than in Washington, D.C.

The Right of the People Peaceably to Assemble

Protecting the residents of the city is the duty of the Metropolitan Police Department (MPD), one of the 10 largest law enforcement agencies in the country. With over 3,800 sworn officers and 600 civilian support staff, the department has a reputation for being tough on crime, and at times, for being tougher than the Constitution condones. In 2000 and 2002, the force showed excessive strong–arm tactics when it reacted vigorously to demonstrations held during the International Monetary Fund and World Bank meetings. In addition to multiple arrests that included non–violent protestors and innocent by–standers, officers shut down approved meeting places and confiscated literature, protest signs, banners, and even medical supplies. Furthermore, they were purported to have fed false information to local media, exaggerating the expected numbers of attendees and potential problems.

The public was outraged. According to Peter Hermann of the *Washington Post*, the ensuing lawsuits against the MPD resulted in $22 million in court settlements. Needless to say, Washington's City Council was less than happy with the overly aggressive and costly behavior of its police force.

Furthermore, it seems that in 2004, MPD was accused of sending undercover officers into protest groups without any justifiable evidence of the groups' wrongdoing. The department also tried to discourage planned demonstrations by making questionable arrests and using other bullying tactics. In his "Foreword" to Heidi Boghosian's "The Assault on Free Speech, Public Assembly and Dissent," Lewis Lapham warned, "For the sake of a vindictive policeman's dream of a tranquil suburb, the country stands to lose the Constitutional right to its own name."

In response to the expensive lawsuits and bad publicity, the city council passed the "Police Investigations Concerning First Amendment Activities Act," a detailed description of the responsibilities and procedures for investigating activities protected by the First Amendment, which acknowledges the right of individuals or groups to assemble peacefully for the purpose of showing support for a social, political, or religious cause; protesting; counter–protesting; and demonstrating. The new legislation was designed to provide specific guidelines for the MPD to balance ensuring public safety with protecting the Constitutional rights of individuals.

Washington City Council's 2004 Statute included another necessary and important provision: It required the Office of the Auditor of the District of Columbia to monitor the police department's compliance to these guidelines. Yearly reports to the Council from the Chief of Police were to be examined by the auditor and feedback given to the Council and public after a full–file review.

Policing the Police

The Office of the Auditor did not conduct its first audit until 2012 due to budgetary constraints. However, as soon as they received their assignment, a team consisting of an experienced audit manager, an auditor–in–charge, a financial analyst, and a junior auditor signed independence statements, grabbed their briefcases and walked into the MPD. Later in the process, the junior auditor would need to be removed from the case for showing bias. Although the police chief would cite this as a contributing factor to a bad report, proper procedure with transparency was followed to ensure that this issue did not taint the audit.

The purpose of the audit was to determine if, in fact, the officers of the MPD were following the First Amendment investigatory guidelines given to them by the City Council in 2004. Auditors gathered available public information and conducted interviews with in–house management and staff as well as members of other organizations. They reviewed laws, regulations, rules, procedures, and policies and researched investigative practices in light of the 2004 report. Although on the surface it appeared that the department was cooperating, there were problems. It was when the audit team tried to decipher the MPD's record keeping and documentation that issues arose.

In an attempt to protect the identities of its undercover officers, the department had heavily redacted most of the files, documents, and emails given to the auditors. All names, addresses, dates, and locations were covered. In fact, even the names of the specific events and activities being investigated were hidden. While officers appeared to be forthcoming in interviews, there was no way to document the truthfulness of any of their testimony and no way to establish whether or not the MPD was adhering to the First Amendment investigative policies and procedures.

Published in September 2012, the final report for the years 2005–2011 raised serious concerns. The audit found specific issues of non–compliance, primarily in the area of upper–level documentation. The first seven investigative files of 2005–2006 had been totally purged at the discretion of the department. Sixteen of 20 First Amendment investigations were not properly authorized. In 17 undercover investigations, neither written approval nor authorization was on record. Required corroboration statements were missing from files.

Procedures for reviewing and extending approval for three

investigations that timed out at 90 days were missing. Approval to extend two investigations beyond 120 days was also undocumented. Training modules were less than thorough, and no logs were kept to verify mandatory attendance. This raised the very serious question about the preparedness of new officers for dealing with mass demonstrations and other assemblies with First Amendment protection.

The conclusion of the auditing team was that, although the MPD had made some effort to comply, their insistence on redacting key pieces of information in the emails between undercover officers greatly hampered the investigation and left the auditing team unable to verify that the police department was, in fact, honoring the 2004 statutes.

Isn't That Law for Regular People?

Police Chief Cathy L. Lanier, a 16—year veteran with the MPD and an experienced Commander of the Homeland Security division of the department, downplayed the final report. She acknowledged that not all the required documentation was present but blamed the oversight on not fully understanding the extent of the 2004 regulations. Passing off the blame, she suggested that if earlier audits had been done, any inconsistencies would have been immediately addressed. Although she disagreed with the value of the findings, she did agree to implement the 13 recommendations made by the Office of the Auditor. It has also been strongly suggested that the City Council follow up the findings of the audit by conducting an oversight hearing and further review of MPD's compliance. Whether this happens remains to be seen.

Obey the Law When Enforcing the Law

Staying safe is important to Americans, but so are the personal protections guaranteed by the Constitution and the Bill of Rights.

There are established protocols for handling peaceful assemblies, and they are to be respected. Higher–ranking officers should have the wisdom and experience to make investigative choices that honor those protocols. Their signatures of authorization might seem superfluous to some, but documentation is evidence that policies and procedures are followed.

The team of auditors who examined the MPD records concluded that there was significant room for improvement, and the police chief, albeit reluctantly, agreed. When the stakes are so high, as they are in Washington, respecting Constitutional rights is non–negotiable. Sliding down the slippery slope of tiny infringements can very quickly blur the good guys from the bad ones. Watchdogs such as the Office of the Auditor have offered a valuable service to the council and citizens of Washington, D.C.

What is the difference between a taxidermist and a tax collector? The taxidermist takes only your skin.

— Mark Twain

CHAPTER 11

SHELBY COUNTY, TENNESSEE, USA

Rickey Beard was a homeowner who had fallen on hard times. After losing his wife Teresa to cancer in 2003, the 53–year–old veteran began suffering from kidney disease. Rickey fell behind on his property taxes and in 2008, Shelby County seized his home and sold it at auction to a California investment firm for $45,000—just a little over half of what he and his wife had paid for it in 1989. The investment firm then turned around and re–sold the property for $109,000.

'Cause I'm the Taxman

Under Tennessee law, when real estate is seized from the owner for non–payment of taxes and is sold, after the taxes and administrative fees are paid, any balance left over must be placed into a special escrow account until it can be refunded to the owner. In Rickey's case, once his property tax debt was settled and administrative fees were paid, the state owed him a refund of $39,000.

But when Beard petitioned the court for his refund in February 2011, his petition was denied. The court clerk said that the refund had been paid, but Rickey knew he had not received the money. Rickey hired a lawyer, T. Frank Jackson. Upon making some inquiries, Jackson found that Rickey's refund had been paid out the previous June to a company called Sunset Thirty–Three LLC. The case got very interesting when Jackson found that the sole member designated on the corporate charter had the same name, Brandon Gunn, as an accountant working in the county Chancery Court.

Jackson discovered that Gunn was responsible for signing the tax sale refund checks. Armed with this information, Jackson contacted the court's Chief Executive Officer, Wanda Wright, as well as the Chancery Court clerk, Dewun Settle, about Rickey's missing refund.

Settle confronted Gunn over the matter and Gunn admitted that he took the money. He told Settle that it was a one–time transaction in connection with an outside "business" in which he was involved. According to Gunn, Sunset Thirty–Three LLC was a "partnership" that purchased foreclosed homes and ultimately, helped former homeowners recover any refunds due after their properties were sold to pay delinquent taxes.

Settle should have fired Gunn for the corruption and should have reported his conduct to the police or prosecutors. Instead, Settle advised Gunn to return the money. Gunn agreed to do so. In a letter dated February 17, 2011, Gunn stated that he had no direct contact with his business partners, but admitted, "It was a dumb mistake." He added, "I fully understand the conflict of interest now." About his company, he wrote, according to the *Memphis Daily News*, "At this time the group is dissolved. They are in the process of putting the funds back into the court due to my involvement. I ask for understanding and grace during this process. I do understand that there will/or may be other ramifications."

Gunn was as good as his word: between February and April, he started to replace the money he had taken. However, as subsequent investigations revealed, the methods Gunn used to make good on the missing funds were counter–intuitive, to say the least.

Be Thankful I Don't Take It All

As is the case with virtually all public institutions, the government of Shelby County, Tennessee, must undergo yearly independent audits to ensure that all monetary transfers are accounted for. In their 2011 audit report, the accounting firms of Watkins–Uiberall and Banks, Finley and White noted a "significant deficiency" in the way the Chancery Court was handling its financial transactions due primarily to a "lack of segregation of duties and lack of management oversight."

Specifically, the auditors noted that:

- the same person who did the paperwork was also authorized to sign the check;
- low–level clerks were allowed to sign checks, regardless of size;
- there was virtually no supervision or accountability; and
- account balances were not being reconciled with the general ledger properly.

Furthermore, there were checks issued without the required judge's order and some checks went out without any supporting documentation at all. Some checks referenced properties reported as sold for back taxes, but official records of these sales could not be found.

The clincher, however, is that the most recent report was not the first time auditors had noted these problems and made recommendations to deal with them. In fact, these problems had been highlighted every year for the previous *five* years! Failing to address these findings was corrupt and provided an opportunity for dishonest employees in Shelby County government to steal money.

Given the opportunity created by this corruption, it isn't too surprising that over $1 million ultimately went missing.

One for You, Nineteen for Me

By the time Rickey Beard's attorney finally smelled a rat and called Dewun Settle to the carpet over his client's missing refund, Brandon Gunn had been very busy indeed. Initially hired in 2005, Gunn had been a less–than–stellar employee, according to his evaluations. On at least three occasions, he made careless errors that resulted in cash shortfalls. One incident resulted in a two–day suspension in December 2007. The following year, he allegedly engaged in an inappropriate relationship with his immediate supervisor, Veronica Nelson. According to several reports, the two exchanged rather steamy emails while on the clock. Furthermore, Gunn showered her with money and gifts, no mean feat on his public servant's salary of not even $30,000 a year.

It was about the same time that Gunn set up his business, Sunset Thirty–Three LLC. He also apparently used another business entity, First Family LLC, but no corporate charter or even business location for First Family has ever been found.

By the time Settle confronted him over the misappropriation of funds in February 2011, Gunn had funneled almost $1 million into his business accounts. Over the next two months, however, Gunn went through his "process of putting the funds back into the court" by stealing an additional $90,000.

Don't Ask Me What I Want It For

It would tend to decrease corruption if the Chancery Court notified former homeowners of any refunds they are entitled to receive, particularly since many of those refunds run into the tens of thousands of dollars. Such a notice would be meaningful and would have resulted in more taxpayers getting the refunds to which they are entitled. However, the Chancery Court had no obligation to notify people losing their homes to tax sale that they were entitled to anything, nor even to attempt to locate them. The burden rested on the former homeowners to petition the court for their refunds. As a result, refunds often sat in accounts, unclaimed, for months or even years, creating an opportunity for culpable employees. It was these old, unclaimed refunds that Brandon Gunn went after.

Tennessee law provides an opportunity for the former homeowner to reclaim his or her property. Property owners who can pay the amount they owe to the county within one year after the sale can have their property returned to them. When this happens, the purchase price is refunded to whomever bought the property, and the entire deal is off. This process is called "redemption" and contributed to Gunn's opportunity to siphon so much money out of county coffers without attracting attention.

Investigations by internal auditors as well as the county commissioner, the State of Tennessee and ultimately, the FBI, revealed a scheme that was almost elegant in its simplicity. In one transaction, a property was sold at auction in May 2009 in order to cover delinquent taxes in the amount of just under $11,000. The successful bidder paid $51,000 for the home. After back taxes and court fees were deducted, the former homeowner was entitled to the remaining $40,000. This amount was placed in the escrow account vulnerable to Gunn.

Gunn waited just over a year after the sale. In June 2010, when title to the foreclosed home officially passed to the new owner and the old owner had not shown up to claim the refund, Gunn wrote a check to his shell company, Sunset Thirty–Three LLC for $40,000. No one else reviewed the payment. No one ensured that the payment went to the former homeowner. The escrow account wasn't even reconciled.

Brandon Gunn made thirty–seven similar transactions over nearly three years.

He might have pulled it off for a lot longer had Rickey Beard not shown up with a lawyer. Gunn was not particularly subtle about his new found, ill–gotten gains, however; in addition to giving gifts and money to co–workers, he treated himself to a grand lifestyle that included weekend trips to San Francisco and Miami, and traveling to see his favorite football teams playing around the country.

It turned out, however, that Gunn was not the only one involved, and not the only one with something to lose.

Declare the Pennies on Your Eyes

Court clerk Dewun Settle had an opportunity—and an obligation—to fire Gunn and report the embezzlement in February 2011. Yet, Gunn continued in his employment for an additional two months, stealing an additional $90,000. Settle said nothing about it to anyone until September. At this point, Shelby County Commissioner Michael Ritz started asking Settle the hard questions. Settle blamed budget cuts that had reduced his staff by almost a third for the lack of oversight.

Still, it seemed that Settle, as well as Veronica Nelson and Wanda Wright, were primarily concerned with covering their behinds. Ultimately, Ritz filed ethics complaints against all three that alleged they tried to cover up the incident.

All parties connected with the scandal resigned from their jobs. In October 2011, Brandon Gunn pleaded guilty to charges of embezzlement and money laundering. He and a co–conspirator were sentenced to four–year prison terms. Upon his release, Gunn will remain on probation for another three years.

In the meantime, Gunn's culpability and the corruption of Shelby County government resulted in its insurer, Travelers, paying for 90% of the losses. Brandon Gunn has repaid a paltry $83,000. Even after those losses have been recovered, taxpayers have had to cover over $98,000 in further losses.

Woe unto them that decree unrighteous decrees, and that write grievousness which they have prescribed;
To turn aside the needy from judgment, and to take away the right from the poor of my people, that widows may be their prey, and that they may rob the fatherless!

— Isaiah 10:1–2 (KJV)

CHAPTER 12
HOPEVALE UNION FREE SCHOOL DISTRICT, NEW YORK, USA

Some thieves hold up their victims with a weapon or threat of physical force. Others rob their victims with a pen or a computer.

The latter kind of thief may not be a career criminal, but just an opportunist. He or she may be a fundamentally decent human being. Given the right circumstances however, when placed in a position of trust and presented with temptation, this person will take advantage of the opportunity. These actions betray that trust, but the betrayal is not usually immediately apparent to the victims. Eventually however, someone in an organization will notice that something doesn't add up.

This is what happened in the quiet community of Hamburg in western New York.

Saving the Children

Young women and girls who were abused, abandoned, or orphaned had few options in the mid–nineteenth century. A few years before the outbreak of the American Civil War, a group of Roman Catholic nuns established Our Lady of Charity Refuge in the city of Buffalo, New York. Their purpose: to offer these young women protection and assistance by providing food and shelter. Eventually, the Refuge offered job training, education, and child care services.

After 125 years, the Sisters moved their facility to the nearby town of Hamburg, where the rural surroundings would be more conducive to their work. When plans for educating their residents away from the facility fell through, the Sisters decided to bring the school to the residents. In 1971, the facility was renamed "Hopevale" and was made part of the Hopevale Union Free School District.

Eventually, Hopevale became a Special Act school district—one of eighteen public school districts in New York charged with the task of serving at–risk youths. The facility was able to provide services to over 130 young people with a history of neglect and abuse. By 2002, Hopevale had achieved recognition from the Council on Accreditation (COA), a prestigious international organization that establishes best practices for child and family service programs around the world.

Small, But Effective

Although the Hopevale school district was publicly funded with tax dollars, it was run differently from most public school districts. Normally, property owners understand that the public schools their community's children attend are financed in part by a levy, a special tax that is voted on by residents. Furthermore, schools and their operations are usually governed by members of a local school board, whose members must run for election periodically—just like any other elected official.

This was not the case with Hopevale. Because its purpose was to serve a small population of at–risk youth in an eight–county region, it was funded in part by the school districts from which Hopevale's students had come. Additional funding came from sales tax revenue, grants, and the state of New York. The seven–member school board was not elected. Five of the members were appointed by Hopevale, Inc. while the other two were appointed by the New York State Education Commissioner. As with other school districts, a superintendent worked with the school board to oversee and manage the school district's day–to–day operations, including financial transactions.

Hopevale school district had an operating budget for the 2005–06 school year of $3.7 million. Almost 85% of this budget was designated for "personal services, employee benefits, debt service, and interfund transfers," according to a report from the New York Office of the State Comptroller. Compared to large school districts in major metropolitan regions, it's a modest amount. One might understand why the school board and the superintendent were willing to allow one person to have complete control over the district's finances, particularly a trusted employee who had been with the district for many years.

Sticky Little Fingers

All public school districts are required to undergo regular audits of their finances. This is standard operating procedure, and Hopevale was no exception. A private accounting firm, Fox & Company, LLC, examined their financial statements annually. Normally, the purpose of this type of audit is to simply verify that all the numbers add up.

In 2006, superintendent David Frahm was informed that the

numbers were in fact *not* adding up. Nearly $200,000 seemed to have gone missing. Dr. Frahm decided it was time to bring in the big guns from the Office of the Comptroller of the state of New York.

Initially, the New York Comptroller investigated financial records spanning a relatively short period of time between July 2004 and October 2006. However, as the auditors dug deeper into the district's financial records, more discrepancies surfaced. Eventually, the investigation was expanded to include records dating back to July 1999. Among their discoveries:

- Over $55,000 had been paid to a retired principal and two teachers.
- $39,000 in "retirement incentives" was unreported.
- A $5500 "sick leave bonus" was added to an employee's salary instead of going toward medical expenses.
- Unauthorized salaries, totaling $10,700, had been paid.
- An extra $1000 was added to a teacher's aide pay envelope.

That was just for starters. And there was only one person who was in a position to make it happen: business manager and longtime district employee Ken Mangione.

Too Irresponsible to Be a Babysitter

A report issued by the Comptroller in July 2007 stated that responsibility lay heavily on the Hopevale UFSD. According to the report, the school board:

- had no policies or guidelines in place regarding the handling of finances;
- failed to supervise the financial processes, including the use of computers;
- did not require back–up documentation when checks were signed; and

- did not consider the risk of such a thing happening.

It also turns out that Hopevale's private accounting firm had not done its job very well. Primarily however, it all goes back to the fact that the school board had placed all control of district finances in the hands of one person, Ken Mangione. He had no supervision, and nobody working with him who might have kept him honest, or at least blown the whistle.

Please, Sir, I Want Some More

Under normal circumstances, Mangione could never have gotten away with his embezzlement for so long. One reason his thefts went undetected was due to the lack of controls over the district's computer information system. Normally, accounting software used by businesses and organizations will not accept conflicting data, such as a payment that exceeds an authorized, pre–determined amount. Such programming can be overridden, of course, but in most cases, this would require some kind of protocol or password known only to certain supervisors. Furthermore, execution of such overrides usually requires authorization from more than one person. Having sole control of the processes, Mangione was able to override these controls with impunity. He needed no authorization and had nobody looking over his shoulder.

And there was no way for the staff working in the business office to know what was going on.

As the auditors closed in, they found that Mangione had written himself checks with special codes that included "retro" (retroactive), "per diem" (daily expenses for travel, meals, etc.) and "cont–adj", that is, continued adjustment—basically, Mangione was giving himself raises. They also found checks that had been issued off the books—including one for $1500 that was reported for "consulting services" that had never been delivered.

When Mangione was finally caught dead to rights, he was summarily fired from the job he'd held for 35 years. Arrested in December 2006, Mangione was eventually hauled into court, where he entered a guilty plea on two counts of grand larceny. When asked by Erie County D.A. John Dosher where the money had gone, Mangione's reply was short and simple: "It's at the casino."

Ken Mangione had a gambling addiction as well as some issues with the Internal Revenue Service. He was a frequent visitor to casinos at nearby Niagara Falls, throwing money down on both sides of the border.

On March 2, 2007, New York Supreme Court Judge Penny Wolfgang sentenced Mangione to six months in prison and five years probation. In addition, he was ordered to undergo addiction treatment and repay $50,000 (the amount not covered by Hopevale's insurer) to the district over the next ten years.

Hopevale Does Not Spring Eternal

In the wake of the audit, superintendent Dr. David Frahm and the school board implemented new procedures and safeguards, based on the comptroller's recommendations, helping to ensure that Hopevale and the school district would not fall victim to such theft again.

Sadly, the school's days were numbered. Although the facility's COA accreditation was renewed in 2007, Hopevale's residential program ceased operations at the end of the 2010–11 school year, 155 years after a group of nuns started their work to make life a little less difficult for abandoned girls and young women. Fortunately, the Hopevale UFSD was able to combine operations with the neighboring Randolph UFSD, which was also organized under the state's Special Act covering at-risk youth. Fifty faculty and staff members were able to keep their jobs, and the children continue to receive needed specialized educational services.

On the state level, the Hopevale embezzlement scandal was just one of many that, in the words of state comptroller Thomas DiNapoli, himself a former school board member, "threatened public confidence."

These scandals led to the passage of new legislation providing regular, thorough audits of all school districts, charter schools and educational services agencies in order to help "prevent fraud and mismanagement from the inside [illegible] ensuring that school district officials have the information and understanding they need to recognize and prevent existing or potential fraud and abuse."

Putting Ken Mangione in jail did not save Hopevale. The corruption that the school board allowed was not corrected by pointing the finger of blame. The school board did not provide adequate internal controls. The independent auditors share some blame, too. Even a little supervision can make a big difference.

Grandmother was lying there with her cap pulled down over her face and looking very strange.
"Oh, grandmother, what big ears you have!"
"All the better to hear you with."
"Oh, grandmother, what big eyes you have!"
"All the better to see you with."
"Oh, grandmother, what big hands you have!"
"All the better to grab you with!"
"Oh, grandmother, what a horribly big mouth you have!"
"All the better to eat you with!" And with that he jumped out of bed, jumped on top of poor Little Red Cap, and ate her up.

— Jacob and Wilhelm Grim, *Little Red Riding Hood*

CHAPTER 13

KING COUNTY, WASHINGTON, USA

Yes, it's as you always suspected. There are public servants who lean over the counter, look left and right down the halls to make sure that nobody's coming, and snag a few $20 bills for themselves out of an unlocked cashier's drawer. Even if they steal small amounts, over a period of time, the numbers can be devastating to the public entity.

Usually, embezzlement consists of two parts. The first part is the obvious one: take the money. But the second step is just as important: fix the records so that the money isn't missed. If the thief leaves a paper trail, the scheme won't last very long.

A common scheme that is difficult to detect is to swap cash that has been recorded with checks that have not. A customer pays with cash, which is recorded, placed in the till, and a receipt is given. Later, another customer pays with a check. No receipt or a false or reprinted receipt is given. The check is placed in the till and the cashier takes the exact amount of cash. The check is not recorded. At the end of the day, the till balances, so there is no record of the theft.

In Washington State, one recent audit identified a "volunteer supervisor" making off with $3,000 in gate proceeds from the Kitsap County Fair. In another audit, a caretaker in Thurston County put the "five–finger discount" on $7,000 in grave opening fees. Another $2,500 was "liberated" in team registration fees paid at the South Kitsap Parks and Recreation District. These are common crimes. The amounts stolen are typical.

Beach Boys 'Go Granny Go' Department

In 1997, an auditor noticed that certain Highline Water District bank deposits did not match up correctly with customers' utility bills. When he went and asked the accounting clerk about it, she broke down and confessed to pocketing the cash receipts that had been paid at the counter.

The auditor started chasing down the errors. Management at the District was totally cooperative. They took hold of this loose string on the sweater, and pulled, and the entire sweater came apart. Around 8,000 utility customers had been affected by the theft of $357,000. They assured the press that the clerk was fired. Same day, even.

The clerk was a 62–year–old Renton woman who (this should

start to be cliché by now) was well liked by her co–workers."Grandma," they called her, and obviously she inspired grandmother–level trust, since she was in charge of all the cash with no supervision to speak of. Even the most basic internal controls require some separation of duties, but no one watched what Grandma was doing.

Friends, as well as the minister at her church, insisted that she was a very caring person willing to help anyone. Fourteen people wrote to the judge, pleading for mercy on Grandma's behalf. Grandma was remorseful in court. She pleaded for mercy. She told the judge that she "struggles daily" to figure out what motivated her to steal the money. The judge was not impressed. Obviously, Grandma stole the money so that she could spend it, just like someone eats a carton of ice cream before bed because it tastes good or uses drugs because it makes them high.

The judge ignored the maximum 3–month sentence for first offenders and sentenced Grandma to thirty–three months for the "enormous amount of work and vigilance" that went into her struggle to figure out why she would possibly want $357,000.

If It's Nobody's Money, Nobody Is the One Watching It

The Highline Water District's internal controls were perhaps a skosh behind the security you find at your local bank. Each day, Grandma received a huge bag of cash and checks from the cashier at the pay window. Grandma then processed all of the payments into the computer system. Grandma prepared the bank deposits. Grandma took the deposits to the bank. And she even reconciled the accounts with the bank statements.

With clinical language, audit report diagnosed the technical ailment, "inadequate segregation of duties." This is a little like saying that Fidel Castro's government was light on checks and balances or smoking does not improve the lungs. Grandma wound up fired and prosecuted, but the interesting thing is that Grandma's immediate supervisor, the finance manager was fired also. He no doubt had some nervous moments before finding that he wouldn't be prosecuted. He may not have been culpable, but the corruption was too significant to let it slide.

If you're wondering about technical–type details, Grandma's lapping scheme was to pocket cash collections and hide the theft by using later payments to credit old account balances. And customer feedback was routed to—well, you can guess which water district employee.

Grandma's eyes were big enough to see bogus account numbers she needed to create. Her ears were big enough reconcile the huge shortfalls. And her teeth were big enough to chomp out some special computer codes allowing her authority to adjust accounts where needed.

DAMAGE REPORT, SCOTTY!

Grandma's good works at her local church offered little solace to Peggy Bosley, Highline Water District manager. Ms. Bosley stated that Grandma's embezzling scheme caused massive strife and conflict with customers for years afterward. "Our credibility is shot," she moaned. How would you like to be the HWD representative on the phone, telling one of your 70,000 customers that their bill is actually correct? Steve, do you mind taking calls today?

The judge handing down the jail sentence also ordered Grandma to repay the money, but as a practical matter, she won't make a dent in her debt. "I think she'll pay $150 a month, and that's the last we'll hear of her," prosecutor Scott Peterson said.

The water district worked for years to make up the $357,000, of which only $75,000 was covered by bond insurance. They cut various programs to save money and dropped two paid positions.

An Ounce of Prevention Is Worth Three or Four Hundred Grand

Grandma swiped $357,000 in two years and three months. But the monthly cash hemorrhage is easy to count up: $12,000 to $13,000 per month. About $3,000 to $4,000 per week was vanishing into thin air—er, into cookie baking apron pockets.

So how much does a good auditor cost? Is it less than $12,000 per month?

It's not like the water district's cooked books were difficult to find. 8,000 accounts were doctored. Grandma confessed immediately when she was told there was a problem. The amount of time that Grandma continued her scheme apparently would have been curtailed with either more frequent or more thorough audits.

If you have a great auditor and she were to catch a problem in the first year, she will have paid her own salary for several years. Even better, frequent audits would actually prevent the theft from ever happening. In fact, studies show that auditing for theft easily pays for itself.

Corruption wins not more than honesty.

—William Shakespeare, Henry VIII, III.ii

CHAPTER 14
WILLAMSON COUNTY, TENNESSEE, USA

A person who works for a government agency generally has a job that offers reasonable pay and benefits, as well as a certain amount of job security and employee protection. For many of us, that would be more than enough.

It wasn't for Kerraina Jensen, however.

The Baying of the Bloodhounds

Jensen was hired as a bookkeeper for Williamson County Animal Control District (WCACD) in 2000. For ten years she performed her job dutifully and adequately. At least, that's how it appeared.

Then, in late March 2010, a notice arrived from the Tennessee State Comptroller's office. The county Office of Accounts and Budgets (OAB) reported that a $356 deposit from the WCACD had gone missing. It's not a huge amount, but it was more than could be attributed to simple accounting errors. It was enough to raise a red flag.

This small shortage resulted in an investigation that included an audit of all receipts from WCACD over a five–year period. The audit compared receipts and deposits made with the OAB. In many cases, receipts were issued that showed cash was received, but nothing was ever deposited.

There was only one person who had been responsible for dealing with those transactions. Almost the same day, Kerraina Jensen admitted to stealing the money and submitted her resignation. Within six weeks, she signed a confession.

She Knows Where All the Bones Are Buried

In addition to keeping the books, issuing receipts, and making the deposits, Jensen was also responsible for employee timecards and payroll records, including her own. It turned out that she had been careless about recording employees' hours properly, and although an electronic system was used, Jensen frequently used a pencil on her own timecard. She was thus able to pad her hours with impunity, claiming to have worked through lunch and compensating herself for unauthorized personal time off. Director Tony Fortner told the State Comptroller that he had "checked them for accuracy" and had given "verbal approval" for such "timecard adjustments." However, the state auditor's rebuttal noted that the "adjustments" in question lacked "adequate supporting documentation." Fornter had relied on Jensen's word. Furthermore, leave forms did not specify the amount of time Jensen had taken for personal reasons (medical appointments, school functions, and so on), and there was no way to know how long she had actually been away from her duties while still on the clock.

Investigators learned there were numerous holes in the system at WCACD. For example, employees were able to freely use each other's personal identification numbers for things like accessing the county fuel pump in order to fill up their own personal vehicles. County vehicles had specific fuel cards for this purpose. However, when the county disposed of an official vehicle, the associated fuel card had not always been deactivated. Former employees were still listed as authorized to use these fuel cards, and it's a safe bet that they did. Again, Jensen had been sloppy in her duties; she had rarely bothered to reconcile fuel receipts with billing statements from the county's supplier.

The bottom line: Kerraina Jensen had been given too much control over too many different functions that should have been carried out by separate people. Segregation of such duties is a system of checks and balances that any well–run business, organization, or government agency should have in place. The WCACD did not. In fact, the WCACD had been in violation of state law, which requires county officials to make deposits within 72 hours of receiving public payments. Failure on this score helped to enable Jensen's theft over the five–year period in question.

The State Comptroller placed the responsibility squarely on the shoulders of those who should have been supervising Jensen: the "lack of segregation of duties is the result of management's decisions and is a significant deficiency in internal controls that increases the risk of unauthorized transactions," according to the final report.

The entire debacle ended up costing the taxpayers of Williamson County an official total of $106,446.17 over a five–year period. That does not include $27,419.52 that Jensen may have diverted for her own personal use prior to May of 2005. Unfortunately, the State Comptroller was unable to review those receipts, as they had long since been destroyed. Nor does it include the salary she received when she was paid for not coming to work.

In November 2010, Kerraina Jensen was sentenced to eight years in prison. The sentence was later commuted to probation, however, and she was ordered to make restitution. However, as of June 2012, she had yet to repay a single dime.

Leader of the Pack

A thief has no one to blame but himself or herself. But citizens can blame not only the thief, but also others who could have prevented the theft and did not. When a thief makes off with thousands or even hundreds of thousands of taxpayer dollars, there is often someone who was too trusting, who failed to put sufficient controls in place, and who provided the perfect opportunity for the less angelic side of human nature to assert itself.

On a ship, the captain is held responsible for the actions and behavior for the crew. When Tony Fortner, director of Williamson County, Tennessee Animal Control, submitted his resignation in September 2010 in the wake of the Kerraina Jensen case, county mayor Rogers Anderson insisted that Fortner had done an excellent job, and that the embezzlement had nothing to do with the resignation. Speaking to a local newspaper, Anderson said, "If I thought Tony was involved, he would have been terminated."

Certainly, Mr. Fortner did not steal public funds. But the State Comptroller's report issued a month prior to Fortner's resignation found that "several weaknesses contributed to the opportunity for the cash shortage [embezzlement] to occur and could not be detected currently by management . . . management did not adequately segregate duties among employees . . . nor provide sufficient management oversight."

There is no reason to believe that Fortner was anything besides a good–faith player who wanted success for Williamson County generally and for Animal Control specifically. But, as director, Fortner was responsible to make certain all the numbers added up and nobody was dipping into the till. Fortner was responsible to put into place internal controls that would prevent and detect theft.

Mayor Anderson told a TV reporter that the county tries "to hire good people that are honest people . . . people that you can depend on and rely on . . . we don't hire anyone who's bad. You'd like to think that." No matter how small the town, no matter how close the relationships, no matter how honest or trusted the employees, failing to implement internal controls is a corruption that facilitates culpable behavior.

I hold the maxim no less applicable to public than to private affairs that honesty is always the best policy.

— George Washington

CHAPTER 15

IRA, VERMONT, USA

If you met Donald Hewitt at his place of work, you might take only a passing notice of this quiet, rather nondescript, middle–aged gentleman. His calm demeanor, conservative, gray haircut, and silver aviator glasses could as easily have been suited to a librarian, a friendly guidance counselor, or a congenial member of the clergy.

In fact, Donald was a credit manager for a garden supply and feed company. But he also worked part time as the Treasurer for his hometown, the small community of Ira, Vermont. Since 1977, he had held this responsibility, and for more than 30 years he managed the books from his home office because there was no town facility.

Ira is so tiny it must depend on neighboring communities for its post office, shopping, and schools. Its entire operating budget for 2010 was less than $250,000 dollars, and most of that went to maintaining a truck equipment fund, the volunteer fire department, and tuition for students attending schools in nearby West Rutland.

A Nice Little Community

Named in honor of Ira Allen, the brother of Ethan Allen who fought with the famous Green Mountain Boys in the American Revolution, this little farming town sits just southwest of the city of Rutland. It is home to about 125 families spread across 21.4 square miles, all connected by a maze of winding dirt roads. Each fall brings a line of flatlanders who come to leaf peep as autumn colors decorate the landscape, but for the remainder of the year, Ira goes pretty much unnoticed, just like the part–time town Treasurer.

Donald Hewitt enjoyed meeting people at work and getting to know new folks who moved into the area. In fact, he took special pleasure in being able to help those who were delinquent with their tax payments. He went out of his way to help them, often waiving late fees completely. His parents and family faithfully attended the local Baptist church and were held in high regard in the community. He and his wife raised two children in a modest, raised–ranch house resting on just an acre of land.

Donald Hewitt no longer lives in Ira. Today his home is a tiny cell in a federal prison. He is completing a 27–month sentence for embezzling more than $348,000 from his friends and neighbors back home. After that he will have three years of supervised release, during which he can start paying restitution. His home was confiscated and sold at auction, although it only brought in $79,210.51 and the final purchaser was the town itself. His apologies at the annual Town Meeting Day in March 2010 came too little and too late. While some church members were willing to forgive, a majority of angry residents brought a lawsuit against Donald that won them a $1.1 million judgment. It's safe to say that Donald Hewitt's life will never be the same.

How Did It Happen?

Three ingredients are necessary to create the perfect opportunity for embezzlement, and unfortunately, Ira, like so many small towns, was ripe for such criminal activity.

First, Donald Hewitt was a highly trusted individual. He and his family had grown up in the town. He was a true, hometown boy. No one would ever suspect him capable of bald–faced theft. Although Hewitt was questioned about his bookkeeping methods ten years ago when bills were not being paid, trust in his character and in his vague answers overrode further digging into the books. The Select Board, the Town Commission, and the Town Clerk wanted to believe he was an honest man and took him at his word.

Second, Donald Hewitt had the specific skills necessary to manage or to manipulate the town's accounts without being detected. Annual volunteer auditors were unable to discover his thievery not because it was well disguised, but because they lacked the necessary training and skills to complete a municipal audit. Donald actually did very little to cover his tracks. He simply wrote checks to himself from the town's main bank account. He pocketed cash payments and forgave both his own and others' tax bills, writing off as "paid" those that were not covered. Because he had not only full control of all the books, accounts, and bank statements, but also guarded sole access to them in his own home, Hewitt was able to fabricate monthly and annual reports for the Town Board.

Third, embezzlement is difficult to detect when individual transactions are small. Because property taxes, cemetery fees, and other payments were relatively small, it was not difficult for Hewitt to transfer money back and forth between accounts to pay overdue bills and to keep up appearances.

Eventually, greed overtook common sense, and the money simply ran out. In the summer of 2009, West Rutland threatened to sue the Town of Ira for $291,000 for not paying the tuition of its students. Select Board Chairwoman Christine Tyminski and Board member Karen Davis began pressuring Hewitt to get this bill paid before it became an embarrassing court case. Suspecting the end was approaching, Hewitt tried to make amends by writing the town of Ira a check for $21,951.91. Of course, that was a mere drop in a sizeable bucket of money he had stolen. Unrelenting, the two Board members began looking into the town's accounts. They were horrified to discover barely $100 in the Truck Equipment Account that should have contained almost $50,000. When questioned about this discrepancy, Hewitt simply admitted to taking the money. The police were called, and as word rapidly spread, feelings of shock and disbelief settled over the tiny community of Ira, Vermont. The sadness and anger would follow soon enough.

At the January 2010 meeting, the volunteer auditors strongly recommended that a professional audit was in order to uncover the extent of the damage and all the dirty details. The Board agreed. Forensic Auditor Michelle Cann from the Burlington firm Gallagher, Flynn & Co. soon arrived, rolled up her sleeves, and went to work.

What Did the Auditor Discover?

As a salaried, part-time employee, Donald Hewitt had been authorized to receive $3,600 a year for his services. In actuality, he paid himself at least that amount every month. In 2005, he gave himself an additional Christmas bonus of $3,300. In fact, 2005 was a very good year for Donald Hewitt. He paid himself more than $57,000 that year. He diverted money from the Truck Equipment and Cemetery funds to pay his own tax bill, and others' as well. Without authorization, he forgave delinquent tax bills. He also accepted late payments and changed the dates so that no late fees were added. Hewitt accepted cash payments and credited accounts but pocketed the money. Starting in 2003, perhaps from a twinge of guilt or fear of discovery, Donald Hewitt began occasionally paying back some of the money he was stealing. All together, he wrote 21 checks totaling $57,000.

Because of the lack of records before 1998, the auditor was unable to determine the exact beginning of Donald Hewitt's crime spree, and Donald seemed unable (or unwilling) to pinpoint the exact date either. Based on the paper trail from 1998–2009, Michelle Cann concluded that the loss to the Town of Ira was not less than $693,442. The cost of the audit and legal fees for prosecuting Hewitt would eventually bring the total to a staggering $800,000. The residents of Ira reeled with shock. They were simply dumfounded that one of their own could smile at them in person and then, behind the closed the door to his home office, clean them out financially—year after year after year. They were also stunned to know that they were not alone in facing this kind of problem.

A State-Wide Problem?

Vermonters are fiercely proud of their state, their history, and their way of life. The Welcome to Vermont signs that greet newcomers also boast that this quaint little state has the least crime in the entire nation. What locals may not be aware of is another top billing their state has earned. According to annual studies done by consulting firm Marquet International, for the last three out of four years, Vermont has been among the top ten states in the nation with the greatest propensity for embezzlement.

Several factors contribute to this dubious recognition. A weak economy tends to drive such behaviors. However, living in the midst of a trusting community is also a key factor. Many Vermonters still don't lock their doors at night. Then there is the fact that there are few large businesses in Vermont, and the numerous small ones often have very weak internal controls.

Typical of the national profile, the majority of embezzlement cases that plagued the state in 2010 were perpetrated by women: Office manager Joyce Bellavance, a 40-year employee of Hardwick Electric Department, stole $1.1 million, $700,000 of which went on her Chase Credit Card; Celine Bernier, a 20–year employee at the University ofVermont Extension Department was charged with embezzling $45,000 over a period of several years; and Susan Emilio was caught stealing a total of $750,000 from her place of employment, Lincoln Applied Geology, in Addison County. There's at least one thing you can say for Donald Hewitt: he was not alone.

Can Ira Recover?

Thanks to the recommendations of the forensic auditor, residents of Ira have changed the way the town does business. Without realizing the importance of its decision, the town was already making a smart choice to secure a central facility for Town Office records just before the embezzlement was uncovered. While it was not against any law for Hewitt to keep the town records in his home, it was never a good idea. Today all records are secured in a vault at the Town Office Building.

All mail now comes to the Town Office instead of to officers at their homes, as was the custom in the past. Select Board members verify all bills and payments, and all bank statements have canceled checks attached. Another order of business has been to work the budget to include regular, professional audits.

Recovering lost assets is another matter. The town's insurance company paid out $348,000 to the Town of Ira—money that was desperately needed. Sadly, a greater loss may never be recovered. For this community, trust died when Donald Hewitt's crime was exposed. Not only did he steal money from his friends and neighbors, but he also robbed them of the ability to believe in the inherent goodness in each other. Today, a new level of suspicion hangs over the community, and no one is exempt. Financially, Ira will recover and move forward, but as for emotionally?—only time will tell.

To date, no one really knows what Donald Hewitt did with all that money. His family lived in a very modest home and drove a modest car. They did not splurge on trips, vacations, or luxury items. Large deposits did not show up in his bank accounts. When questioned about the money's whereabouts, Donald's cryptic reply was that he used it "to pay bills." All this leads one to wonder if, in fact, the stolen loot is buried for safekeeping beneath a rock in a field somewhere, or if Donald just frittered it all away, one dollar at a time?

Jerry, just remember, it's not a lie if you believe it.

— George Costanza, *Seinfeld,* Season 6 Episode 6: "The Beard"

CHAPTER 16

MASON, TENNESSEE, USA

If there is such a place as typical "Small Town America" anymore, the west Tennessee community of Mason surely fits the description. Located approximately 20 miles northeast of Memphis, Mason holds fast to its heritage and small–town traditions. One of the major landmarks is Bozo's Hot Pit Barbecue, which has been in operation since Franklin D. Roosevelt was in the White House.

One of those small town traditions brought some big city problems to Mason—from an unlikely source.

Where Everybody Knows Your Name

It is not unusual in small, rural Tennessee towns for almost everyone to know almost everyone else. This is particularly true when it comes to those in public service—such as police officers, firefighters, dogcatchers, and sanitation workers. And public clerks.

Arnita Mitchell was one such public servant. Reverend Tommie Terry, who serves as pastor at Mitchell's church, told a local TV reporter, "I've been knowing her all her life. I know her entire family.

They're God–fearing individuals." Members of the city board said she was "highly respected in the town of Mason."

Arnita Mitchell served her community faithfully and well for seven years. Because Mason is a small, tight–knit community, those for whom Ms. Mitchell worked felt no need to watch over her shoulder. After all, she was a friend and a neighbor, a community member in excellent standing.

What was there to worry about?

Checking It Twice

Audits of city and county financial records by state agencies can be fairly routine, and the Volunteer State is no exception. Tennessee law says that the State Comptroller must "prescribe a uniform system of bookkeeping designating the character of books, reports, receipts and records . . . in all state, county and municipal offices, including utility districts, which handle public funds." Financial records are regularly audited to "determine the extent of the entity's [in this case, the Town of Mason] compliance with certain laws and regulations" that pertain to keeping financial records.

When a team of auditors from the Division of Municipal Audits started examining Mason's records, they noted that money coming in from various municipal fees and traffic citations was duly noted on daily collection reports, but these amounts didn't always agree with deposit slips from the bank. This irregularity triggered an investigation that ultimately revealed a shortage of over $104,000.

Where did it go? And how, as later discovered, did funds continue to disappear over the course of two and a half years?

"This Is Very Embarrassing"

When confronted with the situation, town mayor David Ward was flabbergasted. He had no idea how the money had gone missing, telling the media "You're supposed to go to work, do your job, and be honest . . . apparently, that wasn't happening."

With only two people working in the clerks office, it didn't take long to discover that Arnita Mitchell was the culprit. Making this determination wasn't difficult; Ms. Mitchell was the clerk who actually collected the money. Between the beginning of January 2007 and the end of June 2009, Mitchell managed to make off with over $95,000, help herself and a family member to over $1400 worth of free water and gas services, and award herself vacation pay to which she was not entitled.

Mitchell confessed to the crimes for which she was subsequently indicted in Tipton County Criminal Court. Ultimately, she was sentenced to three months in jail, given eight years of probation, and ordered to pay restitution.

But was justice really done?

It Takes a Village

A corollary to the old saw "it takes a village to raise a child" might be "it takes a community to keep a worker honest." In an ideal world in which every member of a community works for the highest good of all, the trust placed in Arnita Mitchell would be justified. There is no argument about whether Ms. Mitchell was wrong to abuse the trust the community had placed in her. However, whether it is simple greed (as is usually the case) or pressures due to economic struggles in a dysfunctional system that often seems rigged against the "little people," human beings tend to be weak when presented with overwhelming temptation and wide–open opportunity.

In the end, this was the explanation for how Mitchell was able to pull off her scheme for thirty months, effectively stealing $100 from every man, woman, and child in Mason. Blake Fontenay, who runs public relations for the State Comptroller's Office, put it best when he told the *Tennessee Watchdog* that "in a city like Nashville, it is likely she would have had a number of people on her staff. In Mason, [because of the lack of oversight], there was a lot of money she could have taken advantage of."

As the audit progressed, it was discovered that virtually nobody was doing their job. Nancy Hazelrig, the City Recorder, apparently didn't bother to reconcile what was supposedly collected with what was written on bank deposit slips. In addition, Ms. Hazelrig allowed her employees simply to take cash out of the drawer for government purchases; there was no petty cash fund or procedure in place. Neither was there any separation of duties. Ms. Mitchell took money, recorded the incoming payments, prepared the court docket—which tracked the collection of traffic fines—then filled out the deposit slips. Entrusting a single employee with all of these tasks is never appropriate. The fact that Ms. Mitchell was doing it all made it that much easier for her to dip into the till to the tune of several hundred dollars a week for months with no one the wiser. Ultimately, Nancy Hazelrig, who received the lion's share of the blame for allowing the embezzlement to occur, was fired from her position for failing to withhold payroll taxes from the salaries of city employees.

As government is kept in check by the separation of powers, government employees in a position of trust must be kept in check by a separation of duties. This was not happening at Mason's City Hall.

Ultimately however, it is the captain of the ship who is responsible for the conduct and actions of his crew. Mayor Ward said that his town was several years behind on its audits when he first took office in 2007. District Attorney Mike Dunavant, who was part of the investigation, nonetheless called Mayor Ward to task. Dunavant told Memphis TV reporter Justin Hansen that he would be demanding Ward's resignation if the situation was not resolved.

There were those who tried to demand some accountability. Former alderwoman Abbey Cross, who resigned her position and left Mason in the wake of the scandal, told Hansen that she had asked

Mayor Ward why he wasn't signing off on city financial transactions. She said, "The City Recorder is supposed to keep tally of all that, and it was like it was none of our business . . . where's the town's money? Where's it going?"

In response, Mayor Ward advised her to "watch what she said," fearing civil litigation against the town because of the situation.

Closing the Barn Door

Mayor Ward decided to install surveillance cameras as a deterrent and, in an attempt to reassure the townspeople, announced that he was "confident that justice will be served." He told the media that he was "working hard to fix this financial mess" and was determined to do "what's right for the town."

Of course, the horse had already fled the barn.

Since then, the city council has been seeking the services of a private, certified financial professional to handle city finances and is upgrading the city's accounting software. However, as of May 2012, virtually none of the recommendations of the State Auditor had been implemented.

A Job Well Done

While the City of Mason is still attempting to recover from the theft, Tennessee State Comptroller Justin Wilson is pleased with the results of the investigation. Speaking to Nashville journalist Tom Humphrey, Wilson praised his staff: "This is the type of excellent work we expect from our auditors," adding his hope that such cases "will serve as a deterrent to anyone who might consider improperly using public money for private gain."

Dennis Dycus, who heads up the Municipal Audits Division, agrees: "It's only a matter of time before my investigative team catches you. . . abuse of taxpayer funds cannot and will not be tolerated."

It's the financial equivalent of a complete rectal examination.

— Jerry Seinfeld, *Seinfeld* Season 3, Episode 2: "The Truth," talking about his upcoming audit

CHAPTER 17
GARLAND, TEXAS, USA

Sometimes, the crime of theft is a sudden, even spontaneous event. It may even be violent. In many cases however, it's like a malignant cancer that slowly and quietly grows. Years pass before anyone notices.

Patricia Leathers had a decent and very secure job as a risk management adjuster for the city of Garland, Texas. The city was self–insured, which means that instead of carrying a policy issued by an insurance company to cover claims arising from accidents and certain other incidents, Garland maintains its own fund to pay for these losses. Ms. Leathers' duty was to investigate any claims that the city may have to pay. For example, if a city garbage truck collided with John Doe's personal automobile and damaged the vehicle, Doe would file an insurance claim against the city and Ms. Leathers would assess whether the city was obligated to pay. In doing so, she would make sure the claims were valid and settled in a fair and honest manner, just like an insurance adjuster working for a private carrier is expected to do.

Patricia—or "Patsy," as she was known to her friends—also had strong ties to the community. Only a few years from retirement, she was well–liked by her colleagues, described by many of them as a "mother figure." Her husband was a member of the city's police force and had worked for the district attorney's office. People who knew Patsy personally described her as a kind and caring individual; afterward, many of them had great difficulty believing she would betray the trust the community had placed in her.

A New Auditor in Town

Garland, a suburb of Dallas, is the tenth largest city in the Lone Star State. In addition to being self–insured against injury and property damage claims, the city also operates its own public power and water utilities. Over 2000 individuals work for the city, making certain that municipal government operates smoothly and efficiently. Approximately $1.5 million is processed through Garland's financial offices every day.

As one might imagine, keeping track of everything is challenging and costly.

The city government had the foresight to put a significant control in place in the late 1990s. They made the Internal Auditor directly accountable to the City Council rather than the mayor's office or any one department. When they hired Craig J. Hametner for the job in 2007, they found themselves working with a thoroughly trained, experienced professional. Certified as a CPA, a management accountant, and a fraud examiner, Mr. Hametner was not about to let anything get by him. Upon awarding the position to Hametner, city councilman Douglas Athas announced to the public that a number of audits of various departments would be carried out. Among other areas, these included:

- Customer service billing and collections

- Expense reports
- Cash counts
- A follow–up on earlier audit recommendations

An examination of the city's risk assessment was also on the list, which involved the department headed by Patsy Leathers. Councilman Athas assured the people of Garland that

> Just because an area of city government is slated for audit doesn't mean anything is wrong or suspected as being wrong. The audit, of course, confirms proper operation but it also gives opportunity for suggesting better practices and it can identify departments that are performing especially well.

As it turned out, not all was well.

The Adjuster's Gang

Hametner had been on the job only few months when he became aware of suspicious activity. There was a shortage of at least $100,000 that could not be attributed to simple accounting errors. The City Council believed that there had been sufficient checks and balances in place; however, Councilman Athas was forced to acknowledge that "there was enough of a hole in the city's procedures to allow someone on the inside, completely familiar with the payment system, to circumvent detection."

That someone turned out to be Patsy Leathers. However, it turned out that she had had a great deal of outside help—and the losses eventually totaled much, much more than initially thought.

Within a few weeks, it became apparent that the case was going to be far bigger than anyone had realized. Eventually, the Garland Police Department was brought into the case. However, as the investigation expanded, it was like finding a cancer that had metastasized. Not only had the fraudulent activity been going on since the beginning of

1994, there were multiple perpetrators involved, some of whom had no ties to the community whatsoever.

In March 2008, Patsy Leathers, along with a 66–year–old man from Oklahoma named Jerry Don Deviney and 41–year–old Duane Stailey, were arrested on charges of insurance fraud. That wasn't the end of it, however. As more details surfaced about the case, the Garland police called upon the FBI, which ultimately took over the investigation. Eventually, Stailey's current wife Sharon, as well as Patsy Leatherman's younger sister, Connie Powell, and another couple, Kenneth and Leah Brown, were arrested and charged for their participation in the wide–ranging conspiracy.

In addition, the cost to the city turned out to be nearly twenty times the initial estimate. By the time all was said and done, city taxpayers were out over $1.9 million.

Milking the City's Cow

Because Patsy Leathers was solely responsible for processing insurance claims against the city, it was a simple matter to forge claims that could easily pass muster. Councilman Athas later examined some of them, finding "nothing in the paperwork that makes them suspicious." He added that the only way the fraud could have been detected was by "challenging and comparing every detail on the claims, which no city or company could do cost efficiently." According to the FBI report, Ms. Leathers "created false claims for damage and repairs to real and personal property." She then issued checks to her co–conspirators in their names as well as those of non–existent persons. Deviney, Stailey and the others then cashed the checks and paid Leathers her share.

Rustled!

Community reactions ranged from shock and disbelief to outrage. Some people, posting on a community news website, said they could not believe that Leathers or Stailey were capable of doing such a thing. Others, including Stailey's ex–wives and a teenaged daughter, were not surprised; Summer Stailey called her father "a flat–out bum who doesn't care about anyone but himself." A couple of people noticed that Leathers had recently appeared to be living quite well for someone on the city payroll.

Leathers herself finally pleaded guilty in December 2011 and was sentenced to five years in prison. Other members of the conspiracy have received sentences ranging from probation to prison time, and all have been ordered to pay restitution. Stailey, a struggling songwriter and musician who had gotten some support from Jerry Deviney over the years, has expressed regret over the part he played. "I have apoligized [sic] to all who were affected by my actions . . . I have asked for forgiveness from Jesus Christ. I have pled guilty to what I did and deserve to be punished, and will serve my time and make amends for my actions. . . May God Bless you all and the ones that I have harmed or offended in other ways may you someday forgive me."

In the meantime, Craig Hametner recommended several reforms that included separating duties that Patsy Leathers had formerly performed herself, as well as greater due diligence in making certain that all claims against the city have a legitimate basis.

Councilman Athas reported that while Garland, like most municipalities, carries an insurance policy through an outside carrier to cover such losses, the amount in this case may exceed the policy limits. He assured Garland residents, "there are additional avenues for recovery and the city will aggressively pursue each and every one."

Unfortunately, although all perpetrators have been caught and punished, the biggest casualty in the case may be the morale of city employees, the majority of whom are honest and hardworking. Athas says that while the road to justice is a long one, "employee shock and recovery may take the longest."

You got to know when to hold 'em, know when to fold 'em,
Know when to walk away and know when to run.
You never count your money when you're sittin' at the table.
There'll be time enough for countin' when the dealin's done.

— Don Schlitz, The Gambler (1978)

CHAPTER 18

FAIRFIELD, NEW YORK, USA

Although it affects less than five percent of this country's population, compulsive gambling is a $500 billion problem that destroys careers, personal lives, relationships, and families. The majority of gaming addicts are men, but 25 percent are middle–aged women just like 42–year–old Randi Matthews of Fairfield, New York. In the space of a few short years, she drained her town's accounts dry as she nursed her gambling compulsion at the Turning Stone Casino & Resort in nearby Ravena and at Vernon Downs. By the time she was through, Matthews had lost more than $378,000 to casino slot machines. As for Fairfield, the town was about to discover itself in the midst of a financial nightmare.

Green Fields and Green Felt

Fairfield is a tiny hamlet that nestles in the heart of beautiful farmland about 30 miles northeast of Utica, New York. It sits north of Highway 90 and the peaceful Mohawk River. Originally settled by German tenant farmers, it became the "promised land" for New Englanders who forsook rock–strewn pastures for its rich, fertile soil and flocked to the area after the Revolutionary War. Over the years, small farms have dwindled, and most of today's residents are employed in the Mohawk Valley. With a population of less than 2,000, Fairfield has little more to call its own than its zip code and the Hardscrabble Wind Farm that brings in valuable revenue. Residents travel to nearby communities to shop, go to the movies, attend church, or dine out.

Less than an hour away is Turning Stone Casino & Resort, a 3,400–acre enterprise owned by the Oneida Indian Nation. With over 700 guest rooms, an 18–hole golf course, three swimming pools, two spas and several restaurants, this is a first–class, prosperous gaming establishment. Randi Matthews was not attracted by the many amenities this resort had to offer. She only had one reason to make countless trips to Ravena: She needed to be able to feed her growing addiction—Randi Matthews needed to play the slot machines.

Randi's husband, Francis, known as Frank to his friends and neighbors, was the kind of guy people trusted. Electing him as Town Supervisor of the five–member Board seemed to make sense at the time. This position encompassed the responsibilities of both the chief executive officer and the chief financial officer of the town. In short, Frank Matthews was handed total oversight of Fairfield's entire $1.3 million annual budget. After the fact, Randi Matthews would tell investigators that her husband could neither handle finances nor use a computer, a shortcoming that has to make one wonder why he was chosen for this position in the first place. Frank Matthews seemed to concur with his wife's assessment. In court, he stated that he handed the financial responsibilities of Town Supervisor to his wife "because he was not good at that stuff." Perhaps in this situation, not uncommon in small town politics, popularity rather than ability had played a role in the dangerous standard by which community leaders were elected.

You Always Want to Be the House

Randi Matthews had no problem helping out her husband with his town responsibilities. Starting in 2006, she began managing the books, preparing reports, reconciling bank statements, and handling the mail. By 2008, although town members argue the point, she was functioning as Frank's "official" officer/secretary and bookkeeper. That year she was paid $1,800 for her services. It would appear that the Board did approve or at least recognized her role. Until they both resigned in December of 2009, Randi functioned as the Deputy Supervisor but did not draw a salary. There was good reason for that. While the town remained blissfully ignorant, she had been busy cleaning out almost every account.

All Out of Chips

For residents of the northern United States, November is a dark and dreary month. Except for celebrating Thanksgiving and anticipating the Christmas holidays, most days are lackluster and gloomy, as the countryside sighs and settles in for winter. For the Town of Fairfield, this month and the months to follow would be gloomier than most. Word quickly spread that a Board member had just become aware that the town employees' health insurance coverage had been canceled due to lack of payment. How could this be? And why on earth was there only $9,908 in the general fund? It was time to call Thomas P. Napoli at the Office of the State Comptroller in Albany. An audit was in order.

Looking at the Cards

It didn't take long for the auditing team to unravel Randi Matthews' embezzlement scheme and to recognize the Town Board's gross negligence that allowed her criminal activity to proceed unchecked for so long. Because Frank trusted her completely with both the town's and their own personal finances, Randi was free to siphon off money by forging unauthorized checks from Fairfield's accounts, depositing those checks into hers and Frank's bank accounts, and from there, using her debit card to withdraw cash as needed at Turning Stone Casino. Unknowingly, the Board further assisted Randi's thefts by authorizing the purchase of a mechanical signature stamp, which quickly became her favorite tool. It was just that simple.

State auditors pored over bank statements, cash receipts, and bank transfers dating back to January 2004. Monthly reports were measured against bank statements. The minutes of Town Board meetings were carefully studied, and local officials and employees were interviewed. A separate town account for Fairfield Fun Days was too confusing and undocumented to sort out at all. In short, Fairfield's financial standing was nowhere near the fabrication that Randi Matthews had created and maintained for the last three years.

How had she pulled this off? Because Randi had unlimited access to the town's funds without any form of supervision, she had total freedom to write unauthorized checks to herself and to Frank and to manipulate the books to cover her tracks. Monthly and annual reports to the Board were altered to present normal–appearing financial dealings and were never accompanied by telltale bank statements. Bank reconciliations were either ignored or fabricated. Randi opened incoming mail before her husband or Board members could see it. She signed unauthorized checks with the stamp bearing Frank's name and listed those check numbers as "voided." She also dipped into the unsupervised Fairfield Fun Days Account. What started as a $939 theft in 2006 mushroomed to more than $378,000 in just three very short years.

Everyone Has a Tell

The audit clearly helped Fairfield residents and the Board, in particular, recognize that they too had some culpability in this unfortunate situation. Failing to provide proper oversight or maintain internal controls had left the door to the chicken coop wide open. The most fundamental issue of management, keeping executive and financial duties segregated, had been ignored. Giving the Supervisor absolute and unmonitored responsibility was negligent and irresponsible, regardless of the reasoning. Randi Matthews used that notorious, Board–approved signature stamp 316 times to write unauthorized checks to herself and her husband. If the Town had simply scheduled regular audits to verify its accounts, the thievery would have been detected back in 2006 when Frank's wife was just getting started.

Breaking the House

Five months after the State Audit, county prosecutors used this information as well as other investigatory findings to visit the grand jury. In April 2010, Randi Matthews was arrested and charged with 350 counts related to theft. After initially pleading "not guilty," she changed her mind and accepted a plea deal. Matthews was sentenced to 13½ years at Bedford Hills Corrections Facility. She was also ordered to pay restitution. She will be eligible for parole in 2014. Throughout the trial, both Randi and Frank maintained that he knew nothing of her gambling addiction or the illegal activity she used to support it. He was not charged. Townspeople have their own opinions about his level of innocence.

For the Town of Fairfield, Randi Matthews has taught them an expensive and sobering lesson. Not only did she clean out the coffers, but she left the town heavily in debt. Fines and late fees from unpaid IRS bills for 2008 and 2009 would total $10,000. Interest on unpaid loans would add another $45,825 to the debt load. Unpaid health insurance premiums had caused the cancellation of employee policies. All told, the town had to borrow $200,000 just to get caught up. The final tally placed the new debt load above the $800,000 mark. Fortunately, revenue from Hardscrabble Wind Farm was available to offset some of this unexpected expense, and the board hoped to leave resident tax rates alone, at least for the immediate future.

Residents of the Town of Fairfield expressed feeling victimized by Randi Matthews' behavior. They also felt that the town's good name and 200–year history had been forever tarnished by this notoriety. However, not given to holding grudges, at election time, with the exception of Frank Matthews, the same Board members were reinstated. Valuable suggestions made by the auditing team have been given serious consideration and changes made. Hopefully, important lessons have been learned from this experience.

Good name in man and woman, dear my lord,
Is the immediate jewel of their souls:
Who steals my purse steals trash; 'tis something, nothing;
'twas mine, 'tis his, and has been slave to thousands;
But he that filches from me my good name
Robs me of that which not enriches him,
And makes me poor indeed.

— William Shakespeare, Othello, III, iii

CHAPTER 19

NASHVILLE-DAVIDSON COUNTY, TENNESSEE, USA

It is Christmas Eve of 2007 in Nashville–Davidson County, Tennessee. Everyone has gone home from the Election Commission Offices to celebrate the holidays with friends and family. Even the security guard is missing. No one thinks about two Dell laptop computers that are left out and accessible. After all, one is broken and the other is in the process of being tested and purged of confidential information.

There is no alarm system. The security camera is unplugged. There is no security guard. A rock crashes through a first floor window. A shadowy figure enters the Election Commission building, grabs the laptops and some other portable gear and disappears.

Although another guard would later mention noticing a raised window, no one reported anything amiss until December 26 when the unusual coldness of the building prompted further investigation. It didn't take long to discover that a $3,000 router, a digital camera, two radios, and several employee–owned musical CDs were missing. Most importantly, also absent were the two laptop computers. At least one of them contained all the names and Social Security numbers of every one of the 337,000 registered voters in Davidson County. Although both laptops were password–protected, Metro Elections Administrator Ray Barrett admited, "any smart computer user likely could break the password." None of the highly sensitive information was encrypted.

The Value of a Good Name

There is a market for the identifying information of real people. Those 337,000 names and Social Security numbers could have been sold as many as 30 times and fetched a sale price of $5 each. In the right hands, they could have been worth more than $50 million dollars. The Metro Government had no choice but to immediately notify all affected persons that their identities were at risk and that they should monitor their financial affairs especially closely in light of this serious breach in security. The mailing expense alone was $150,000. Since it had to assume full responsibility, the Council also offered to provide each victim with one year of identity–theft protection, purchased through Debix Identity Protection Network. At $10 per account, the total cost of this mistake was potentially millions of dollars. The cost of encrypting all sensitive information with protective software would have been as little as $15,000. It was an expensive and embarrassing lesson.

As it turned out, the thief cut himself entering through the broken office window. Robert Osbourne, recently paroled from a 2004 sentence for stealing in Marshall County, was quickly identified through DNA matching. Homeless and down on his luck, he was more interested in turning a few dollars than he was in identity theft. At least one hard drive was recovered later in January, but the damage to people's trust in their local government's security systems had already been done, and recovering that would take time.

The Davidson County theft is only one example of the corruption of not properly protecting sensitive information stored on computers and other portable pieces of equipment. Laptop thefts have caused serious breaches at the Chicago Public School Systems, The Gap, and AT&T. In 2010, almost half of all lost or stolen laptops were reported to contain sensitive information. Only 30 percent of those computers were encrypted, and only 10 percent had any anti–theft technology installed. Theft or loss of sensitive information is the most frequent cause of stolen identities. Paul Stephens, director of policy and advocacy with the Private Rights Clearinghouse, states that "as many as 217 million U.S. records were exposed from 2004–2007 alone." According to the 2012 Data Breach Investigative Report, "Most data–breach victims fall prey because they possess an often easily exploitable weakness," a situation that a simple information technology audit could prevent. Furthermore, a 2012 IT Audit Benchmarking Survey also found that only 65 percent of organizations schedule yearly IT risk–assessment audits. Fully a third of smaller organizations (less than $100 million in annual revenues) have never conducted any type of IT assessment—just like the Elections Commission in Davidson County.

The majority of computer thefts in 2004–2007 were, like the Tennessee robbery, simple targets of opportunity, and, unfortunately, a shocking 96 percent of them were also easy marks with relatively easy access. In the United States in 2011, data–breach incidents cost organizations an average of $194 for each compromised record or about $5.5 million per company. The average lost laptop had an associated cost of $49,246, the majority of which was represented by the lost data. Simply encrypting the information would have reduced that figure by at least $20,000.

Back to Davidson County—on the same day that citizens were notified of the serious security breach, Mayor Karl Dean called for a full–scale IT security audit of every Metro department. It was obvious to all that there were two primary concerns: the physical availability of the laptops was unacceptable and the sensitive information was not adequately protected.

By May 2008, the "Limited Review of Information Systems Controls for The Election Commission of the Metropolitan Government of Nashville and Davidson County" was completed. An experienced IT audit team had reviewed the existing procedures already in place to safeguard all sensitive electronic information at the Elections Commission. They also analyzed other selected and general applications controls and made recommendations that included asset management, application security practices, and disaster recovery planning.

Concerning sensitive materials, the audit suggested limiting login access to only entry–level rights that were necessary for performing specific tasks. Employees should be brought up to date on IT protection procedures, and the Metro IT Department should be invited to set and oversee all computer policies for this government office. Standard protective measures should address creating a shield against viruses, encrypting sensitive data, improving back–up procedures, and designing a protocol to ensure physical security of equipment.

The audit supported measures taken immediately after the December break–in. Metro Information Technology Services met with the Election Commission to assist in setting up a more secure system. A website was prepared specifically for those who needed to report potential fraud. Employees were made aware of the importance of following protocols designed to keep laptops and other similar, transportable equipment locked up and out of sight when not in use. Furthermore, the decision was made to stop storing Social Security numbers on mobile devices and other portable storage media. Any employee assigned to a laptop computer was given awareness training and a specific, unique login.

Davidson County learned a very expensive lesson from the corruption of failing to protect its information technology infrastructure and data. To enjoy the benefits of new technologies, due diligence must be paid to the risks. Just as do other areas, IT needs regular audits to help prevent a recurrence of this kind of unfortunate and expensive event. Oh, and as for Robert Osbourne—he's not homeless any more—he's back in jail.

Thieves respect property. They merely wish the property to become their property that they may more perfectly respect it.

— Gilbert K. Chesterton, *The Man Who Was Thursday: A Nightmare*

CHAPTER 20
KOOTENAI COUNTY, IDAHO, USA

George Washington, James Madison, Benjamin Franklin, and the other American Founders set up a government that prevents power from consolidating. The Founding Fathers did not want an agile government. They wanted one that thought about things before it turned a few degrees to starboard or port.

The Founders wanted an ocean liner not a navy P.T. cruiser. They wanted to make it difficult—not impossible, but difficult—for government to make radical changes.

Americans know that checks and balances are important. They are part of what makes America different from the dictatorships we poke fun of in Saturday morning cartoons. We support checks and balances, but it's not easy to understand exactly how those checks and balances work in the real world. Should we spend more tax money on inspectors? Less? Are the checks and balances effective? How much of the taxes a government collects should be spent on programs and how much should be spent on monitoring that the money goes to the right place? How many dollars are we willing to spend to stop a dollar of theft?

Bog Standard Theft by Clerk

From 2001 to 2010, a deputy clerk named Sandra Martinson in Kootenai County, Idaho embezzled $139,000. Auditors caught the clerk just before retirement, when they went over the county checkbook and spotted a long string of suspicious payments made to Mortinson in even–dollar amounts, $350.00 and $900.00 and $425.00. Normal bills collected by the county, of course, had cents figures ranging from $0.01 to $0.99. All 212 of the checks to the clerk ended in $.00. As auditors noted, almost all of the normal, appropriate debits and checks were for odd figures.

The auditors also found that Kootenai County checks to other entities were always hand–signed by Martinson or by Dan English, her subordinate. But the even–dollar amount checks to the clerk were all signed using a signature stamp of English's signature.

Martinson's attorney asked for probation based on the fact that she'd had no prior convictions. It is common, even routine, for a first conviction to carry a light penalty. Prosecutors and judges understand that some people make a misjudgment, but if it isn't habitual, society and the demands of justice can be satisfied with a lenient sentence. In this case, however, the misjudgment occurred 212 times over the course of ten years.

Public Trust Doctrine

The day before her sixty–third birthday, Martinson was sentenced to 90 days in jail. A theft worth $139,000 should draw a serious penalty. But suppose it had been $10,000? What sentence would we give then? Is it the value of the property that we're talking about, or is it the morality that we're talking about?

The Kootenai County Clerk "elected to steal from the public over an extended period of time" in a "systematic scheme of stealing," First District Judge Fred Gibler told the embezzler at her sentencing. "Public servants are held to a higher standard when we're dealing with public funds."

Auditors defend an idea that is basic to democracy—that certain resources belong to the public, not to powerful individuals. This is known as the "Public Trust" doctrine.

Can a king own the seashore? The Roman emperor Justinian was the first to answer this correctly. Certain things in the world can never belong to a Caesar, he said. Even a man–god cannot own the air, the sea, or the seashore, and therefore no Caesar can forbid a man from approaching the sea to wade in it. Some things, no government can legitimately touch.

Imagine that the city of Chicago sold the waterfront of Lake Michigan to a large corporation, and then the corporation decided to charge for the privilege of walking up to the shore of the lake. As you know from other chapters, you are probably thinking that if this is Chicago, you probably don't have to imagine. In fact, the state of Illinois actually tried to do this once, selling land under Lake Michigan to Illinois Central Railroad. The U.S. Supreme Court threw this transaction out as a violation of the state's public trust obligations.

No city or state, said the Court, can deny citizens the right to "enjoy the navigation of the waters, carry on commerce over them, and have the liberty of fishing therein freed from the obstruction or interferences of private parties."

Local governments, and the officers and employees that run them, allocate assets that are held in trust for the benefit of the people. As trustees, public officials have very high duties to protect these assets. These duties include scrupulous honesty, avoiding conflicts of interest and self dealing, and providing all the information that matters to the public. True, $139,000 in tax money isn't exactly the sand on the seashore. But the principle is the same. Citizens rely on—they trust—government to hold resources for the people.

When the people lose confidence in government, bad things happen. There aren't a lot of governments around that are more than 200 years old, as the United States is. Most of them run into public hangings, beheadings, and civil wars a lot sooner than that.

When we say we "trust" our government, we mean that we believe it will fulfill its policies, projects, and promises appropriately, efficiently and within a reasonable time. Just as locks help keep honest people honest, auditors help keep trusted officials trustworthy.

Transparency Is Not Just a Hologram

So what did Kootenai County do to prevent the next clerk from swiping another $139,000? The auditors' recommendations focused on *transparency*. Transparency is a grand theme in the audit world. To understand auditing and inspection, we need to understand the idea of transparency.

Kootenai County's new clerk, Cliff Hayes, worked for over 20 years as a police chief. He brought in a former bank fraud investigator, Jim Simmerman, to restore the public trust through auditing. Simmerman was the type of auditor who could really light a fire under people's chairs. When Simmerman worked in the banking industry, Hayes said, "He would knock on the bank's door at 7 o'clock in the morning and everyone inside would panic. He went to any bank that they were suspecting problems in."

Simmerman's reviews focused on transparency. They wanted to know, said Hayes, "where is cash coming in, how are we counting it, [and] do we have two people doing it? He's going through all the steps . . . I want to figure out that we're doing everything right."

Transparency in government occurs when officials are operating in a way that makes it easy for non–officials to see what actions are being performed. If a cashier makes change at the counter, and separates the bills, and puts the change openly on the counter, the customer can verify the transaction. Transparency in local government works the same way. It should be easy for the public to see what is going on with the their money.

"It's hundreds of items and the explanations on it are not clear to me and they are not clear to the commissioners," Hayes said. "It should say what it was, who it's for, when we bought it, how much it is. When I can't understand it, it needs to be fixed."

As other illustrations in this book point out, elected officials don't always know what is going on. Government finances can be complex, and accounting methods may be so corrupt that they can't understand it if they try. But former police chief Hayes said that his goal wasn't just that the government's transactions are transparent enough that county managers can understand them. "I want the average citizen to know what it means."

Auditors' recommendations very often focus on the same theme.

When a state trooper passes you on the highway at 70 MPH in a 60 MPH zone, does it bother you at all when he pulls you over another time for doing 66? Does the trooper believe that 66 MPH endangers the public, or doesn't he?

Ultimately we want troopers to do a good job keeping our roads safe. Similarly, we want county clerks to do a good job distributing money so that the public can drive on safe roads and to their destinations, including those the county supports, such as hospitals, libraries, or offices We want officials who believe in what they're doing—that's the only way they'll do a reliable job of it.

In the 1720s, there was no police force in England. A man

named Jonathon Wild became a celebrity in London as the "thief taker," a bounty hunter who turned in the most criminals.

But it turned out that Wild himself was actually the top figure in organized crime in London. He could catch criminals because he knew them all. If a criminal angered Wild, he would bring a posse of thugs and turn the man in, collecting the bounty in the process. His purpose was not to prevent crime for the benefit of the public, but to control crime for his own benefit, and he used public resources to do it.

This was a good deal for Wild, but not exactly something for London to be proud of. London officials decided to organize what is essentially a team of auditors—a paid police force. They decided that if citizens hand control of public resources to government officials, it would be preferable for them to be part of the solution and not part of the problem.

Every public official, not just auditors, has a duty to eliminate corruption. Every imperfection or inadequacy that can be eliminated should be eliminated. Eliminating corruption does not always require a determination that someone caused the corruption, sometimes it's just there. But public officials have fiduciary duties to use their best efforts to eliminate corruption, not enrich themselves at the public's expense, and to provide all the information that matters to the public. Those duties include having auditors formally review the records to ensure all the rules are being followed.

Money is the worst currency that ever grew among mankind. This sacks cities, this drives men from their homes, this teaches and corrupts the worthiest minds to turn base deeds.

— Sophocles

CHAPTER 21

NASHVILLE-DAVIDSON COUNTY, TENNESSEE, USA

Information technology allows us to process more transactions faster and more accurately. Databases allow all the necessary information to be stored. Electronic processes can complement physical processes to reduce the risk of lost money and to promote the proper handling of transactions. But none of it works if you don't set up the software to do it.

And sometimes, even with checks and balances in place, individuals still manage to find holes to exploit.

Nashville, Tennessee, is probably best known as the home of the "Grand Ole Opry" and the center of the country music industry. However, it is also home to numerous colleges and universities as well as museums (hence its other nickname, "Athens of the South"), large health care and research facilities, and more. The city's primary occupation, however, is government and law. Nashville is the state capital, and the city itself is consolidated with Davidson County. The Metropolitan Government of Nashville and Davidson County provides services and law enforcement for over 625,000 people.

Local citizens pay taxes on real and personal property, vehicle licensing fees, and utility fees to the Office of the Trustee. To process all these transactions, Metro Trustee Charlie Cardwell had nearly thirty people working under him. The Trustee's office implemented the usual internal controls. For example, the Trustee assigned each assistant his or her own cash drawer. Each cashier had an individual ID and a password to access the software used to process payments.

At the end of each workday, each cashier accounted for every cent deposited into his or her drawer that day. The cashier made sure the balance matched the figure on the daily report. Once this balance was completed, an administrator also balanced the receipts.

Like all new employees, Kenneth Fleming Jr. was restricted by the software to certain basic transactions when the Trustee hired him in August 2004. He was allowed to accept payments and enter the amount into the system, using his own unique ID. He could also reverse a transaction—that is, he could mark payments as having been refunded or mark transactions as not completed—until the transaction was posted.

Fleming apparently did his job well. In the spring of 2010, he was given administrator rights over the computer software used to process payments. Among other things, this allowed him to adjust the amount of a tax assessment.

It was a golden opportunity, and it took several months for anyone to notice that something wasn't quite right.

In 2011, Deputy Trustee Gerald Grigsby ran across some unusual transactions. Specifically, Grigsby saw a number of reversed transactions that were done for no apparent reason and traced them to Fleming's user account. A cashier in the trustee's office might reverse a transaction for any number of legitimate reasons. For example, a property owner may have successfully appealed the assessor's valuation, or a taxpayer's check may be returned for insufficient funds. However, there seemed to be no reason at all for the reversals that Fleming had done. In some cases, a property owner's tax liability had been reduced to nothing.

Grigsby's discoveries triggered an internal audit in the Trustee's Office. The audit revealed two distinct types of transactions. Two–thirds of the reversals, totaling around $123,500, had been covered by subsequent payments, but a third of them—amounting to nearly $92,000—had never been repaid.

Grigsby took his concerns to Cardwell, and the two of them confronted Fleming over the missing funds. He readily admitted to embezzlement. Fleming was fired from his position three days later. Cardwell contacted the District Attorney soon afterward and a month later he filed a report with the Tennessee State Comptroller's Office.

Fleming's scheme was essentially to rob Peter in order to pay Paul, himself being Paul. The State Comptroller's report uses audit jargon to describe Fleming's method as a "lapping scheme." Fleming would pocket one citizen's tax payment, then pay that citizen's taxes with the next incoming payment. This way, Fleming showed 99 of 151 related transactions were paid and the $123,500 has been accounted for. However, the other 52 transactions—where Fleming simply zeroed out the taxpayer's liability—allowed Fleming to walk away with almost $92,000.

Fleming managed to carry off his scheme despite some internal controls being in place and rather sophisticated software with its own controls. When the Tennessee State Comptroller issued his report, he noted that Fleming was able to "make adjustments to account balances while simultaneously maintaining custody of one of the office tills." In other words, Fleming could report that he had collected a certain amount, and because he was handling the cash drawer, there was no way to confirm that his report was accurate. The Trustee should have required that two separate individuals carry out these functions. In addition:

- There was no official process for making adjustments to taxpayer accounts.
- There were no regular reports reviewed by management that would ensure that adjustments were authorized.
- There was no process for dealing with payments on delinquent tax accounts.
- Cashiers were able to post–date transactions entered into the database (in other words, accept a payment today and record it as paid in the future).

One implication here is that the Trustee's office relied heavily on its technology, but they set up the electronic processes for efficiency, not control. The feeling may have been that having the software and requiring every cashier to have a unique user ID and password in order to access the database was sufficient. It appears that this did allow Fleming to be identified as a thief quite easily. The problem is that while modern computers are remarkable machines capable of carrying out diverse tasks precisely, they cannot make value judgments. A computer can only do what a human programmer has instructed it to do. The Nashville–Davidson Metro Trustee's office had a good system. They simply failed to use it effectively. In the words of the State Comptroller, the problems resulted from "a lack of sufficient [software] application controls . . . and poor management oversight."

Cardwell has assured property owners that their "status . . . is secure," adding that the Trustee Office "consider[ed] their balances paid in full," even if the payment was stolen. In the meantime, he and his staff were working with their insurers to recover the stolen $92,000.

Even if the money is recovered, a more serious consequence of this corruption is the erosion of trust that people have in their government. Strong internal controls ensure that governments handle the money appropriately. Handling the money appropriately leads to a government that makes a difference. And that leads to public confidence. But it takes a long time. The loss of $92,000 is worth much, much more then the mere money to a government, which always needs the confidence of the people.

Because power corrupts, society's demands for moral authority and character increase as the importance of the position increases.

— John Adams

CHAPTER 22
ERIE COUNTY, OHIO, USA

The whole town agreed, Tamara Holeton was an excellent employee. According to newspaper reporter Richard Payerchin of *The Morning Journal,* Ms. Holeton had received excellent reviews on her work in the Erie County, Ohio, Treasurer's Office. Her supervisor, County Treasurer Jo Dee Fantozz, told the paper that Ms. Holeton "was always on time, pleasant speaking on the telephone, helpful to customers, pleasant and helpful to fellow employees and keeping busy."

That was in 2008. Two years later, Tamara Holeton was a disgraced former employee facing ten years in prison. And the taxpayers of Erie County were out nearly $150,000. To make a bad situation worse, the county government was facing a special—and very costly—audit. In fact, the cost of that audit would ultimately exceed two-thirds of the amount that had gone missing.

An Unlikely Suspect

The job of a county deputy treasurer is to collect money

received by other county departments—such as property taxes, sale of dog license fees, building permit fees, and so on—and record the amounts collected and balance the accounts at the end of the day.

Prior to being hired for this position in 2001, Tamara J. Holeton had worked in retail and banking. She obviously had experience when it came to handling money, and people who had known and worked with her spoke highly of her. For nine years, her work performance had been nothing short of stellar. It came as a major surprise to her supervisor and co-workers that, when the balance sheets came up short at the beginning of 2010, evidence pointed to Ms. Holeton.

When Ohio State Auditor Mary Taylor started looking into the matter in February of that year, neither she nor the people assisting her in the investigation had any idea just how much money was missing. But Ms. Holeton's supervisor, Ms. Fantozz, indicated that the losses could run into five figures.

Where It Started

The trouble seems to have started in 2005, when the Erie County Treasurer's Office switched to a different accounting system. The problem with the new system was that it lacked a way to reconcile the County Auditor's balance sheets with those of the Treasurer's Office.

In essence, the county's right hand had no reliable way of knowing what its left hand was doing.

In August 2009, the county decided to move to yet another new system that would include some controls that were lacking in the current system. The switch was scheduled for January 2010. In the meantime, the Erie County Auditor's Office decided to get ready for the changeover. They contacted the State Auditor's Local Government Services (LGS) division. This is part of the state auditor's office that assists municipal and county government agencies with bookkeeping when necessary. In this case, the objective was to help Erie County to make sure all the books were in order and the figures were adding up before adopting the new bookkeeping system as data was transferred to the new system. It should have been a routine audit.

It wasn't.

The Investigation

When LGS started looking into the matter, it discovered that figures entered in the accounts receivable columns weren't lining up with those on the deposit slips. Furthermore, as the investigation progressed and the audit was expanded, LGS found 250 payments received at the county treasurer's office over an extended period that for some reason never made it to the bank. The problems, not coincidentally, had started in 2005, when the county treasurer's office had switched to its current system.

It didn't take Fantozz long to trace the problem to her star deputy. When finally confronted over the issue in February 2010, Holeton confessed almost immediately. She was summarily fired, but that wasn't the end of it. The treasurer knew there was money missing. What Fantozz didn't know was how much. And finding out was going to prove costly.

The Price Goes Up...and Up...

Initially, the reconciliation process involved in transferring county financial records from its current system to the new one was going to cost approximately $22,000. After Holeton's embezzlement was discovered, however, Fantozz called upon state auditors to do a special investigation in order to determine how much she had stolen. The price tag: $70,200. That was on top of the cost of the original data transfer. Fantozz attempted to reassure the commissioners that it was only an estimate, and that not all of that amount might be necessary.

That was in May 2010. Later that summer, as the auditors finished going through county records with a fine–toothed comb, the bill had gone up by an additional $40,000.

By the time all was said and done, Erie County paid $111,000 to find out that Tamara Holeton had pocketed $146,592 of taxpayer money.

The Why of It

According to a 2010 report on embezzlement issued by Marquet International, Ltd., a security consulting firm, the typical embezzler is a female in her early forties working in a financial institution or the financial department of a government agency who has no prior criminal record. Furthermore, the average embezzler is a "sole perpetrator" who has been at it for an average of 4.5 years.

So far, this describes Tamara Holeton pretty closely. However, her motivation was not typical. According to the Marquet report, most embezzlers do it out of sheer greed and a desire to live large. In other cases, addiction is involved, which can include compulsive gambling and shopping as well as drugs. Although "financial woes" is mentioned in the report, difficulty making ends meet is not at the top of the list. It does appear to have been the motivating factor in Ms. Holeton's case, however. Attorney Troy Wisehart, who represented Ms. Holeton when the case went to court, told the *Toledo Blade* that his client was experiencing "significant financial difficulties . . . she was paying her expenses . . . just trying to make ends meet."

It's a sad, but all–too–common story.

Pulling it Off

Ms. Holeton's *modus operandi* was simple. Her job was to count the money in the cash drawer at the end of the day, fill out a "cash out" report, attach the tape from the adding machine and turn it all over to the treasurer, who took it to the bank. All Ms. Holeton had to do was simply to slip some cash into her pocket and forget to turn in the paperwork.

In the meantime, the various departments that made deposits to the treasurer's office kept their own records of what was paid in. These records were kept in a computer database. As long as the old system was in place and nobody looked too closely, Ms. Holeton was able to pull off her scheme. It was when the "paid in" and "cash out" records didn't match—as was discovered during the preliminary audit in the summer of 2009—that Ms. Holeton was finally caught with her hand in the till.

As is usually the case in these kinds of crimes, Holeton was given abundant opportunities by the lack of internal controls and inadequate oversight. One factor that made it difficult to catch Tamara Holeton and determine just how much she had taken was the system itself. There were three cash drawers for four employees. Any cash drawyer could be used by any employee. The drawers were left unsecured during the day, and there was no way to know who had made particular deposits to a specific drawer. Likewise, there was no policy in place to deal with cash shortages or overages. Pay–in receipts were turned in sporadically and were not dated or signed by the deputy who had handled the transaction.

Justice Done?

Tamara J. Holeton pleaded guilty to theft and falsification of documents in August of 2010. At the time, she was looking at a ten–year prison sentence in addition to making restitution. On 1 October, Judge Tyghe M. Tone of the Erie County Common Pleas Court sentenced Ms. Holeton to three years, although she was released after only eight months. Since her release, Ms. Holeton has paid back $49,000 by surrendering her retirement accounts and taking out an equity loan on her home. She will still need to send in monthly payments for years—possibly decades—in order to make full, court–

ordered restitution.

The final loss to Erie County taxpayers, including the special audit that was required, is nearly a quarter of a million dollars. Like most businesses and government agencies, the county has insurance for such losses, but as of 2012, it was not known how much that insurance payment would cover.

[The spirit of party] serves always to distract the public councils and enfeeble the public administration. It agitates the community with ill-founded jealousies and false alarms, kindles the animosity of one part against another, foments occasionally riot and insurrection.

— George Washington, Farewell Address

CHAPTER 23

ISLIP, NEW YORK, USA

In 1991, the University of Washington Huskies football team went undefeated and won the national championship. The head of the football program, Don James, would likely have been elected governor of the state if he had run. He was loved for his victories, and respected for his football program's squeaky–clean reputation.

In 1992, James' squad was again in the middle of an undefeated season and ranked number 1 in the country. After the Huskies crushed the USC Trojans in a famous game, their quarterback, Todd Marinovich, complained, "All I saw was purple out there." Then, as 1992 was sailing along in sunshine and rainbows, the bottom dropped out.

The *Seattle Times* ran a headline on page A–1. It revealed that the Husky quarterback, Billy Joe Hobert, had received $50,000 in unethical loans from an Idaho nuclear engineer named Charles Rice. Suddenly, the entire Husky football program was under fire. A $20 million per year program was at stake, to say nothing of the civic brand that the Huskies lent to the region.

The UW academic administration, not particularly known for being friendly to its own sports programs, audited the football team and imposed significant penalties on itself. It then turned to the NCAA and said, "We've taken care of it." They hoped that their internal audit would deter external penalties.

The NCAA and the Pac–10 conference—to which the UW belonged—were not impressed. The guillotine fell, with a stunning two–year probation of the UW program. Don James, "The Dawgfather," immediately quit. "If they don't think any more of our program than that," James said, "I don't have any interest in being part of this community." The UW football program never fully recovered. The first internal audit was swept away by the external audit. The watchdog system had sharp teeth. University programs got the message: the NCAA would not stop with self–policing.

Who audits the auditor? If the local auditor can't, won't or doesn't do a good job, what is the watchdog process then?

JUST BETWEEN US DEMOCRATS...

In 2010, New York State Comptroller Thomas DiNapoli audited Islip Town cash shortfalls that occurred in 2007 and 2008. A quick scan of DiNapoli's released report might lead you to believe that his New York State office had pulled few punches.

For example, the State criticized Islip Town over its payroll practices. Islip had made numerous unauthorized payments and benefits. In 2007 and 2008 alone, town employees had received leave time, perks, and other fringe benefits worth over $111,000.

On another front, Islip Town had doled out contractor agreements worth over $1.1 million to service providers. None of these service providers was selected through a competitive bid process. There was no way of knowing whether the Town was paying the best price and if it was not, that would be corruption. If the Town was paying a friend or relative of a decision maker too much or the service was of substandard quality, that's culpable.

The audit found that the town charged nearly $10 million of its expenditures to the wrong Town accounts. As a result, taxpayers in Brightwaters, Islandia, Saltaire, and Ocean Beach paid taxes that should have been shared by all voters in the area. This was, or could have been, an attempt to influence elections. Charge the folks whose vote you can take for granted or have written off and curry favor with marginal voters who will swing the next election.

If you think that you've heard this one before, you have: the town clerk did not adequately segregate duties within her office, perform monthly reconciliations of assets to liabilities, perform bank reconciliations, or prepare reports for the board. In other words, cash passed through the pay window and disappeared again without anybody being able to trace what happened to it. This discovery was turned over to the District Attorney's office for investigation.

Storming the Bastille—Well, Standing on the Town Steps, Anyway

So why, when DiNapoli stood outside Islip Town Hall and delivered the report to a small crowd, was he drowned out by protesters who shouted over his announcement? There was a perception that the real pageant was that DiNapoli stood beside his fellow Democrat, Islip Town Supervisor Phil Nolan, and (in effect) delivered Nolan's talking points for him.

"We found a number of long–standing problems in the town that needed to be corrected to prevent future cash shortfalls and unwelcome tax increases," said DiNapoli. "The good news is that the town is correcting these issues," he added.

DiNapoli cleared Nolan of any personal wrongdoing with the phrase "long–standing problems." Nolan had inherited the system, and the moment he realized anything was wrong, he went right to work on it. You may note that Nolan is not the only politician who has taken advantage of this defense. If this defense been made by Nolan's lawyer, it would make for a reasonable—if tired—debate. The problem is that Nolan's attorney didn't present the defense—his auditor did. Whether the audit was biased or not, there was perception that the Democrats were hanging together.

Republican town councilmembers Steve Flotterton and Trish Bergin–Weichbrodt wanted to know why they had to receive Nolan's and DiNapoli's report on the town steps along with other public citizens. Bergin–Weichbrodt accused DiNapoli and Nolan of "white–washing" the report to conceal the real problems—potentially incriminating facts that could indicate that town officials were *deliberately* (culpably) misappropriating funds.

For example, one of the practices that Supervisor Nolan openly acknowledged was to roll over—we might say, "hide"—$10 to 15 million per year in cash surpluses.

The 2008 records showed 214 payments, totaling $24,311,974, that were made *in the last two days of the year.* You read that right. On December 30 and 31, 2008—not usually days on which politicians are known for working overtime—Islip Town paid over $24 million. Of that, $11,839,927 had no purchase orders attached.

As the audit itself stated, an average of $14.3 million per year for three years was "misplaced." This led people to believe that the Town needed more money than it actually did.

Democratic officials blamed it all on long–standing process problems, and protested, hey, our tax rates are the lowest in the area, so what difference does it really make? Republican officials insinuated, darkly, that something much more nefarious was going on, if only it could really be investigated.

Islip Town hadn't stopped there. It had shims in place to shore up failing budget sheets after the fact.

In yet another major budgetary no–no, Islip Town had never bothered to keep funding separate for different projects. When one project ran out of money, Islip simply secured funds for new projects, re–directed the funds back, and left the new project undone. In 2010, for example, Nolan called for a new cash influx of $70 million. "Now Nolan wants to float a $70 million dollar bond to repave the Town and play catch–up with all the things that haven't gotten done, or were not done with the same quality, since we let the Town workers who used to do those jobs go," remarked Town Councilman Steve Flotterton, a Republican. "There is already $141.3 million dollars in bonds that will come due within the next ten years, according to Town records. How will our children be able to pay for that and then another $70 million?" Flotteron asked.

And so, after the New York Comptroller's friendly audit, business ran as usual.

Distracting Public Councils, Enfeebling Public Administration

Comptroller General DiNapoli's audit showed there was corruption in Islip Town's finances. DiNapoli went outside the finding of corruption and stated that there was no culpability, or at least that Mayor Nolan was not culpable. The Republicans claimed that there was culpability and supported their position with evidence that the audit had not unveiled all the corruption, reasoning that this must be because DiNapoli and Nolan were both Democrats.

DiNapoli may have been influenced by the spirit of party to diminish the power of his audit by expressing an opinion about culpability. The audit found and quantified corruption. That was powerful. It should then have been up to others, including, perhaps, the Town Council and prosecutors, but certainly the voters, to determine who was accountable for these failures. By affirmatively supporting Mayor Nolan, DiNapoli lost credibility. His audit lost its objectivity. The whole mess got messier.

But an audit should not be expected to find all the problems. There was enough in the audit to make voters question whether Town finances were being handled correctly. Questions of financial policy are political and should be submitted to the political process. The Republicans on the Town Council wanted more. They wanted an indictment of political decisions that had been made. In other words, they wanted the same partisan advantage that Mayor Nolan wanted.

Audits can have political consequences. But an auditor must not try to control the political consequences. To do so jeopardizes the public confidence in the audit, the auditor and the audit process. Audits must instead be fair, objective, and supported by evidence. The politics will take care of themselves.

If absolute power corrupts absolutely, does absolute powerlessness make you pure?

— Harry Shearer

CHAPTER 24

CASS COUNTY, MISSOURI, USA

In 2012, Cass County Auditor Ron Johnson filed a complaint against County Clerk Janet Burlingame. Shortly after, the Cass County prosecutor filed a legal action to remove Ms. Burlingame from office. The infractions might not have made the local police blotter—Ms. Burlingame's husband and son had been hired to transport voting machines. They'd been paid a total of about $5,500 and $1,600, respectively, over the previous eight years.

The case reads like an Ethics 101 term essay for college undergrads. It's against the rules to hire your spouse. But everything in life is simple if you reduce it to just one principle. Is it relevant that Johnson is a Republican and Burlingame is a Democrat? Was the audit actually a thinly disguised political food fight over voting–process disputes?

A full–blown government audit can cost anywhere from $10,000 to $100,000 or more. Suppose Ms. Burlingame knew better, and thumbed her nose at the system. You still have the question: would it be worth spending a hundred grand to punish nepotism that cost the government, at most, $7,000?

The Cass County prosecutor was not slow to come to a conclusion on the case: "The Missouri Constitution prohibits acts of nepotism by elected officials, and the Missouri Constitution states that you forfeit your office." Well, that's simple enough. You've got to uphold the law.

The public reaction is likely to be on the other side of it, though. America seeks a government of the people, by the people, and for the people. This is the kind of story that can anger the public, perhaps even poison it against auditors. To many, it will sound like a well–meaning mistake on the part of a nice lady who didn't even realize she was doing anything wrong. And the husband and son probably did it for less than someone else would have. In the backs of our minds, we all dread the IRS representative at the door, casting a long shadow, grim smile on his face and a "Gotcha!" on his lips.

Nepotism for Fun and Nepotism for Blood

Are we talking about crime and punishment here? What is nepotism?

In many parts of Europe, helping your friends and family with your little slice of power is admired. Nepotism is literally seen as a virtue. What kind of jerk wouldn't share the fruits of life with his friends? One European commissioner, giving a job to her dentist, demanded angrily "Are we supposed to employ only people we don't know?"

In France, Jacques Chirac's chief publicist was his daughter. In that country, appointed committees are often loaded with mistresses, with grandnephews, and with pals of chums and homies of buddies. They don't think anything more of it than you would worry about writing a letter of recommendation for a friend in your local church.

So with "mild" cases of nepotism, a husband who made $5,000

over ten years, are we talking about a cultural difference, just a matter of taste? Maybe we're not talking about good and evil.

On the other hand, suppose you're talking about a County Sheriff who hires 1,500 totally unqualified friends into well–paid law enforcement jobs. When you think about the cop responding to your 911 call, it becomes a little easier to see the problem with government staffing choices being based on personal relationships.

Triage Department

Not all corruption is the same. When you rush to the emergency room with internal bleeding or a dislocated elbow, you don't want to wait in line for two hours behind people who have sore throats. Neither do the doctors want that. That is why doctors use a "triage" process. They sort the patients according to urgency, and they sort them without apology.

A good auditor will bring the same sense of proportion. The major expense of an audit program is the payroll cost. So an audit executive wants to get as much meaningful work completed as possible. Over any given period, an audit team can do a finite number of audits. She wants bang for the buck! She has to exercise her discretion wisely. She wants to eliminate the most serious corruption, to deter the most dangerous behavior, to protect the most valuable public assets, and to help create the healthiest government possible.

So, she can't afford to select a case merely because it's an easy win, or because a particular violation gets her hackles up. She is there to keep government healthy, and she needs to pick her battles with good judgment.

Proceed to Level 201 Scan

In the movie *The Terminator* the killer robot scans its targets quickly with Level 101 Scans. When the Level 101 scan identified targets with a higher priority, the robot proceeded to a Level 201

Scan. Government auditors are not looking to target victims for termination, but an effective Level 101 Scan can go a long way towards building a reputation for a reasonable and smart audit office.

Auditor Johnson might have given Clerk Burlingame a quick phone call, rather than beginning a formal exchange of paper. (Perhaps he did; we don't know for sure.) Clerk Burlingame might then have chattily explained, oh, yes, of course, we needed the machines moved quickly and my husband was the only person available when we started that. Was that a problem?

Although we don't know how the conversation may have gone, when an auditor calls to discuss the matter more informally, the process can be expedited. If she receives testimony that is credible and forthright, the auditor might be able to determine that the case is not high priority.

Sometimes the auditor can fix a problem by showing his teeth just a bit, by securing agreement to repair the situation, like a busy District Attorney who pleads out a reckless driving case if satisfied that the driver has been scared straight. The auditor might then often be able to move on to cases that are more deserving of public scrutiny.

The Accidental Auditor

If we fly over the government at 30,000 feet, we see that auditors and inspectors are there to promote effective government. In some cases, up to 40 percent, 50 percent, even 60 percent of tax dollars are siphoned off through fraud. In many cases, critical government functions are performed weakly because jobs were handed out to people who just flat shouldn't have gotten them.

In 1931, Clessie Cummins was coming down Cajon pass in California when the brakes went out on his truck. He almost didn't survive the white–knuckle ride down the pass. After that, he developed the idea of an engine brake—the "Jake Brake"—to back up the wheel brakes on heavy trucks. When a loaded semi–trailer comes down a mountain, the trucker doesn't want to hear the screech that tells him his brake pads are fried. If he does hear the screech, he's awfully thankful for his "Jake Brake." A runaway truck needs a backup line of defense.

In 1776, the Founding Fathers were braving of King George's wrath when they devised a government with checks and balances on it. Those checks and balances have worked.

Whether an auditor saves a lot of money with an audit, or whether he doesn't, his function as "check and balance" goes to the very root of our democracy. Sometimes it might seem like the audits aren't having much effect. However, in the grand scheme of things, that audit department is limiting the capacity of other organizations to misuse tax dollars.

In a perfect world, the auditor leaves the government in better shape than he found it. His audits lead to justice against real misdeeds. In the big picture, his audits put a brake on runaway waste and fraud.

Moral Compasses and Books of Virtues

What happened to the Cass County clerk accused of nepotism? A circuit judge ruled that Ms. Burlingame could keep her job, observing that "it will be for the electorate to decide, should [Burlingame] seek to stand for re–election for this office, or for any other future office, whether she is worthy of continuing to hold office." Janet Burlingame could keep her job as long as the voters keep electing her.

The Republican auditor could console himself in the fact that he called public attention to $7,000 in wages paid illegally to Democrats, and the good people of Cass County could then make the call.

Should the auditor have been dealing with other things? What would the voters say? Sometimes that is not the worst moral compass for a beleaguered auditor searching for the right direction.

Avoid likewise the accumulation of debt, not only by shunning occasions of expense, but by vigorous exertions in time of peace to discharge the debts which unavoidable wars have occasioned, not ungenerously throwing upon posterity the burden which we ourselves ought to bear.

— George Washington, Farewell Address

CHAPTER 25

VALLEJO, CALIFORNIA, USA

The voters of California passed Proposition 13 in 1978. Proposition 13 limits the property tax that can be charged by fixing the taxable value of a property when it was sold. The fact that the property appreciates over time does not increase taxes. When Proposition 13 was adopted, the voters of California were seeking relief from what they perceived to be an ever–growing tax burden.

On this score, Proposition 13 has been highly successful. According to the Howard Jarvis Taxpayers' Association, the law has saved homeowners in excess of half a trillion dollars over the past generation. On the other hand, the law has created serious cash flow problems for many municipalities, particularly areas such as Los Angeles and the San Francisco Bay region, where property values have increased significantly over the past decade along with the cost of government. Nonetheless, the restrictions on reassessment of property values remain.

One serious consequence has been a shortfall of revenue. This has led to decreases in funding for education, libraries, and other public services that many citizens take for granted. Coastal regions such as the San Francisco Bay Area have been especially hit hard. These consequences started to multiply thirty years later, when the worst financial crisis since 1929 descended upon the U.S. economic system.

Vallejo, California, is the Bay Area's tenth–largest city, located northeast of San Francisco along Interstate 80 on the edge of San Pablo Bay. Calling itself the "City of Opportunity," it was briefly the capital city of California and is home to three major institutions of higher learning as well as to major health care centers.

For the first several years of the twenty–first century, Vallejo experienced what the city's Finance Director described as robust growth. However, according to the Comprehensive Annual Financial Report published in June 2007, there were dark clouds on the horizon. While income from property taxes had been on the rise during the housing boom, other sources of tax revenue—such as sales taxes, motor vehicle registration feels, and utility taxes—had not. The slowing of the housing market did not bode well for property tax revenue, either. Already, the city was feeling the effects of the sub–prime mortgage debacle, which was manifesting itself locally as a decline in home sales and new construction, reducing revenue from taxes and other fees. Skyrocketing oil prices delivered a double whammy to the already struggling municipality. There was also the closing of the Mare Island Naval Shipyard in 1996, which had been a major employer for over 140 years, and the resulting loss of jobs and revenue.

To top it all off, certain provisions of California law—some of which had been approved by voters—had allowed the State government to divert local funds for the use of the state at large.

The warning signs had been there for a long time, and the limit of the community's ability to raise property taxes due to Proposition 13 wasn't the biggest problem. In 1992, a Vallejo Citizens' Committee took a close look at the way the city was handling its finances. The Citizen's Committee warned the city council that the generous salaries for city employees (some well into the six–figure range) as well as retirement and health care benefit costs were not sustainable. They predicted that unless the city council solved some of these problems, the city would be bankrupt within twenty years.

Fifteen years later, an accounting firm in nearby Pleasant Hill was hired to audit the city's accounts Comprehensive Annual Financial Report for the Fiscal Year Ending June 30, 2007. The auditors' report should have sounded the alarms for anyone who remembered the Vallejo Citizens' Committee's dire prediction.

One of the problems with the city's finances in 2007 was that while city financial planners had anticipated some reduction in revenue due to the sub–prime mortgage crisis, they had still overestimated the amount of incoming revenue but underestimated both municipal expenses and the seriousness of the economic crisis. Much of this was due to demands by city workers. According to the report, "the budget assumed significant reductions in public safety staffing levels; however, due to labor arbitration rulings, public safety staffing levels may actually increase."

During fiscal year 2006 the general fund balance dropped by almost half, from $13.85 million to just over $7 million. In 2007, the city was facing a $10 million deficit. The part that was undesignated—in simple terms, the total surplus from all previous years, or "rainy day fund"—had dropped to just over $4.2 million and was projected to run out before the end of June 2008, "unless significant cost reduction or other measures" were taken.

That was in January of 2008.

During the good times when revenues were high and there were actually more public–sector jobs than there were workers to fill them, Vallejo—like many other California communities—offered generous contracts to police, fire, and other municipal workers, including very nice benefits and retirement packages. When the economic storm came, the city was still locked into these contracts. But it was going to be difficult, if not impossible, to pay these workers what they had been promised. In fact, compensation for firefighters and police accounted for approximately 80% of the budget.

Help Me, Bankruptcy Code, You're My Only Hope

On May 6, 2008, just a little more than three months after the auditor projected that Vallejo would run out of money, the Vallejo City Council voted to petition the bankruptcy court under Chapter 9, the part of the law applicable to local governments. Unlike an individual or corporation facing bankruptcy, a city government generally turns to Chapter 9 only as a last resort. As Chicago bankruptcy attorney James Spiotto put it, "The stigma of bankruptcy has the potential to seriously impact a municipality's ability to borrow funds that might be needed to build roads, bridges, sewers, a new city hall or to execute other public improvement projects." Most attorneys who specialize in bankruptcy law would not advise a city to file for Chapter 9.

Not surprisingly, Chapter 9 bankruptcies are rare; since this provision was enacted in the late 1930s, only about 600 municipalities (primarily small utility districts and towns) have filed such petitions.

A large part of what pushed Vallejo over the edge was a number of "unexpected retirements" among the city's safety workers. Suddenly, the municipality was obliged to pay approximately $3.4 million that had not been included in the budget. Earned health care benefits for current and retired employees alone had reached $135 million; to cover these expenses, the city would have to raise an extra $6 million a year in an economic climate of falling real estate values and reduced revenues.

The Unions Strike Back

As Vallejo's bankruptcy went before the court, employees contested the filing, saying that the city government should simply raise taxes in order to meet its obligations to its workers. In addition, city employees argued that the city did in fact have $136 million in cash on hand when the bankruptcy petition was filed. In their challenge to the petition, the unions stated that:

- it was possible to cut unnecessary expenditures in other ways;
- revenue could be raised by selling city property and increasing fees; and
- the city had failed to negotiate with its creditors (including the unions) prior to its filing, and the bankruptcy petition had been filed in "bad faith."

Generally, the workers saw the bankruptcy as a ploy to bust their unions.

The union workers wound up fighting a lost cause; in March 2009, Judge Michael McManus ruled that the City of Vallejo could dissolve its existing contracts with city workers. Citing a 1984 U.S. Supreme Court case upholding the right of the Bankruptcy Court to allow a debtor to "reject any executory contract" (*NLRB v. Bildisco & Bildisco*, 465 U.S. 513), Judge McManus said that public employee unions are not entitled to the same protections under federal law as workers at private companies. However, he did not allow the city to terminate its contracts immediately; instead, he ordered the two sides to go back to the negotiating table.

Ultimately, the City of Vallejo was able to get concessions from two of the public employees' unions; police personnel agreed to reduce their minimum staffing demands in exchange for increases in pay, while installing cameras around the city in order to enable fewer officers to patrol larger areas remotely. Police, firefighter, and management unions agreed to reduced pension benefits for new hires, while health care benefits for retirees and their spouses were to be cut by as much as eighty percent.

In addition, Vallejo's creditors, who were owed just under $480 million, wound up settling their accounts with the city for $6 million.

Vallejo emerged from bankruptcy in November of 2011. As of August 2012, the police department had been cut by over two–thirds, fire protection had been reduced by forty percent, and home values were only about thirty percent of what they were at the height of the real estate boom. Vallejo still suffers from the stigma of bankruptcy, which discourages future investment in the community. Although the city is able to hire workers again, the human resources department is severely understaffed and underfunded, which hampers recruitment efforts. Half of the businesses that once lined the main streets remain empty.

A New Hope

On the other hand, the crisis forced members of the community to come together and take responsibility for their town. Citizen volunteers have formed hundreds of new Neighborhood Watch groups to augment and assist their police force. Vallejo residents voted to approve a one percent sales tax increase in order to help the city meet its obligations and restore services. Although that does not sound like a large amount, it is estimated to raise almost $10 million a year in new revenue. In addition, the city is establishing a new process that will allow the taxpayers to participate in budget decisions.

One woman told a local television station that the bankruptcy was a "blessing in disguise . . . a lot of good came out of it."

Even the fallout from sub–prime mortgage debacle was arguably foreseeable. Michael Lewis, author of *Boomerang: Travels in the New Third World,* has his own take on it. He sees the story of Vallejo as symptomatic and symbolic of a much larger issue of which the sub–prime crisis was a part. He writes:

> The people who had power in the society and were charged with saving it from itself had instead bled the society to death. The problem . . . isn't a public sector problem; it isn't a problem with government; it's a problem with the entire society . . . it's a problem of people taking what they can, just because they can, without regard to the larger social consequences.

Police, firefighters, and city workers perform vital, often dangerous jobs and deserve to be fairly compensated for their services. Governments act through employees and are necessary to make certain a community functions smoothly. But when hard times hit, it is corrupt to block a government's ability to balance its budget. Public service is not about getting rich; it's about public service. In the end, Vallejo, its employees and its citizens were able to think creatively to eliminate corruption.

Giving the government 40% of your money and asking it to make purchasing decisions on our behalf . . . is exactly like giving a passing stranger $50 and telling him to go to the grocery store and buy some stuff for you, except that there is no chance whatsoever that the government will be either honest or a smart shopper. It is absolutely guaranteed that they will steal $20 and waste another $15, give you $15 worth of groceries, and a long, boring lecture on how you should use the groceries.

— Baseball historian Bill James

CHAPTER 26

ORANGE COUNTY, CALIFORNIA, USA

Most citizens who do not work for the government are vaguely aware of the fact that some tax money is wasted. Maybe a lot of it is wasted. But who knows how much? Five percent? Or is it more like ten percent?

However much it is, what do we do about it? A lot of us try to convince ourselves that it is not our problem and that it is okay. There are already watchdog groups out there waging the war. The media is out there, and reporters are piled up three deep who would love nothing more than to catch a scandal. That's what they do. If there is something that can be done, surely they would do it.

After all, we tell ourselves, America is more or less a self–balancing thermostat, right? We learned about it in fifth grade civics class. Whatever can be done is probably being done, we figure. Then we get on with our busy lives.

If you investigated how much tax money is stolen, and how much of it gets siphoned off on the way to where it is intended, and how little is done about it, you would be discouraged. Depending on the program involved, it is not five percent that's being wasted, and it is not ten percent that's being wasted. Especially when government entitlement programs are involved, even half of our taxes may get burned up by the system or pocketed by frauds lying about whether they qualify for the money.

No Good Deed

The California State Auditor praised the Orange County Social Services Agency (SSA) for its efforts in 2008. In cooperation with the State Auditor, SSA established an audit program to detect welfare fraud. The State Auditor determined that SSA saved $1.82 for every dollar spent. That calculation did not take into account the deterrence effect, the decrease in people attempting to commit fraud because they know it is being looked at. These are just first–order cost savings.

If you can get back $1.82 for every dollar you spend per year, how much do you want to invest? Given these results, you would think that the SSA would have quadrupled its anti–fraud spending. Instead, it immediately cut its fraud investigation staff by 34 percent. Without the fraud detection program, SSA then overpaid $9.6 million in fraudulent payments during the next six months, $9.6 million that came straight out of the pockets of authentically needy families.

Busy SSA case managers saw the audit process as a distraction, and cooperation was withdrawn after the immediate crisis was dodged. Certainly, government programs can become too cumbersome and expensive to justify, but this was not such a program. The evidence had been gathered and analyzed. The extra steps that it required were cost effective.

A penny saved is a penny earned. But when it comes to Orange County fraud, let's realize that a penny spent on fraud detection can be a nickel earned, or a dime earned, or a quarter earned. Public support for these audit pennies is a starting point.

When you ask government agencies to police themselves, perhaps by asking their staff to keep the records needed to identify fraud, in theory it should work. But in the government world it often does not work. SSA managers, for instance, may see their role exclusively as completing applications and getting funds to needy families. They tend to see fraud prevention efforts as a hassle, as red tape that distracts them from their jobs.

The SSA has no mention of anti–fraud measures in its mission statement. It does not measure its ability to detect fraud. It does little to no training on the issue. There is no routine examination of the records. When budget cuts are necessary, anti–fraud processes are among the first to go and when they do corruption follows.

Bloodletting

In Los Angeles County in 2006, for example, a grand jury report found that welfare recipients had defrauded the CalWORKS program with a budget of $1.1 billion per year out of—wait for it—$500 million per year. That's almost half of a government budget cow, skeletonized by piranhas that finish their meals unnoticed, unpunished, and that come back the next year to feed again.

A family might not mind paying, say, $1000 in taxes per year to help needy families get back on the path. But are they okay if $400 of the $1000 goes to criminals?

In the commercial world, this would be fraud, but not if it's the government. If someone says, "give me $1000 and I will give you a computer," and then gives you a $600 computer and gives $400 to her brother–in–law, that would clearly be wrong. You would be entitled to get your money back and she may be prosecuted for her crime. But if the government says, "Pay $1000 and we will use it to help the poor like you want," and much of the money goes to someone who is clearly not poor, it is considered normal.

It gets worse. You can choose not to buy the over priced computer. But you can't choose not to pay your taxes, because that may be a crime. Unlike commercial employees, government employees have no material incentive to deliver what was promised—the public must rely on the government's collective ethics, not always a reliable quantity, unfortunately. Often public money simply does not go where it is supposed to go.

However, governments can eliminate the fraud, and often the resulting efficiency is due to the efforts of auditors and inspectors.

Keeping a Finger on the Handout

In Arizona, for example, the state's audit department put in place a fingerprint imaging system so that users would be identified if they attempted to pull duplicate payments. The imaging system itself cost $874,000. They immediately deterred 2,200 cases of fraud, saving a whopping $10 million. Another ten cases of actual fraud were busted, saving another $46,000. The auditing process returned over $10 ($11.49 to be precise) in savings for every single dollar spent. That's like getting 1,000% interest.

Auditors, inspectors, and comptrollers can have that kind of impact, but only if they have the budget and the authority to do something. Ironically it seems like it is *harder* to get budget and authority after an initiative has been successful. You probably haven't found a $1000 mutual fund that returns $10,000 in the first year. But when auditors save money, the response they often get is a budget cut to their operations, as happened in the Orange County case.

If a government agency simply does not address the fact that about 40% of the funds it distributes are not going where they are intended, you can guess what happens. While the process for distributing the funds is streamlined, so too is the system that streamlines payments based on fraud. Fraud is easy under these circumstances. The conveyor belt pouring cash into thieves' pockets ramps up to high speed.

It is not sufficient to keep records. To have an impact on corruption, the records must be examined and the results of the examination must be reported to the public. Until auditors are given authority and budget to do their jobs, no real detection can take place and no real deterrence will happen. A dollar spent on anti–fraud processes can get back ten dollars in detection and deterrence. Culture can change. Government money can go where it is intended. Taxes can decrease without decreasing the services provided.

It's all about accelerating progress—for you and the planet.

— Toyota Prius advertising slogan

CHAPTER 27
SAN MATEO COUNTY, CALIFORNIA, USA

For years, California state and local governments have led America in pushing for new technologies and better regulations to decrease high levels of smog and greenhouse emissions. From 1990 to 2009, the state was able to cut carbon emissions by an impressive 28 percent while coping with a population growth of an additional eight million people.

San Mateo, a peninsula county just south of San Francisco, is one of those determined to take up the fight for clean air. The community bills itself as a "leader in advancing sustainability and green policies and practices." This proactive position has affected changes in everything from land–use policies to building standards to tree propagation to recycling to walking or biking to work.

In 2007 the Board of Supervisors adopted Resolution #069053. This "Cool Counties Declaration" required the county to calculate its contribution to the area's carbon footprint, take inventory of offending contributors, and develop and implement an ambitious carbon emissions reduction plan. The target goals were to reach a regional level of flat emissions by 2010 and to lower 2005 statistics by 80 percent by 2050. Because they are significant contributors to both smog and greenhouse gas emissions, vehicles fell under serious scrutiny in San Mateo, and since change begins at home, the local government decided to go after its own Public Works fleet first.

In September 2008, the Board of Supervisors adopted a follow–up resolution, #069650, which stated that all future compact and mid–size government fleet vehicle purchases must be hybrids or fuel–efficient conventional models capable of achieving at least 30 miles per gallon. The term "fuel efficient" was defined to mean an Ultra Low Emission Vehicle, a Partial Zero Emission Vehicle, or a Zero Emission Vehicle. The goal of this legislation was to increase fuel economy and thereby decrease San Mateo's share of California's carbon footprint by 2012.

The Solution to Pollution

To understand how the Board of Supervisors came to this position, we have to step back a few years and look at a County Auditor's Report from 2003–04. At that time, hybrids were new and exciting. They were projected to be more expensive to purchase but less expensive to operate and maintain and had a higher resale value. Taking into account maintenance, fuel, and salvage value, the County Auditor estimated that the fiscal advantage to owning and driving a hybrid was $1,764 over its life span. Because lightweight vehicles contribute approximately 17 percent to America's total greenhouse emissions and larger hybrids were not readily available, the Operational Review of the Vehicle and Equipment Services of the Department of Public Works recommended a narrow policy that would start replacing only government compacts as they reached the seven–year retirement mark. It was this report that fed the interest of the Board of Supervisors in 2007 and 2008.

The new 2007 and 2008 Resolutions were immediately incorporated into the purchasing policies of the county's Fleet

Maintenance Department, a branch of the Public Works Department, and a strategy was initiated to replace 32 percent of the vehicles in this manner.

Although the figures for the audit report were accurate for the information available at that time, four years later, the Auditor found that the facts had changed. The trade–in value of hybrids was running a significant 23 percent less than predicted, partly because the original figures assumed the vehicles would be sold after five years, rather than the seven–year lifespan that was standard for San Mateo's fleet. Also, based on several factors, including changing gas prices and improvements in conventional vehicles, the cost of ownership for various vehicle models had shifted.

While the Board of Supervisors was sincere in its intention to clean up the fleet, it was also ignorant of the very limited improvement such policy changes would create. In San Mateo County, auto emissions account for 12 percent of the total carbon dioxide pollution. However, the compact division of the vehicle fleet of the Public Works Department of San Mateo is less than 1 percent of the total county's vehicle figures. In the grand scheme of things, changing out 200 conventional cars over a period of eight years for more–expensive hybrid versions was not going to have any significant effect on the atmosphere. Meanwhile, it would noticeably pinch the county's pocketbook.

Here's where it gets tricky. According to the California Air Resources Board, at that time, Honda, Ford, Toyota, and Chevrolet car manufacturers were all producing conventional vehicles that met Partial Zero Emission Standards and exceeded 30 mpg. However, despite this information, the decision was made to buy only costlier hybrid vehicles. Between 2002 and 2010, the department purchased a total of 200 Toyota Priuses and Honda Civics and seven Ford Escape SUVs—all of which were hybrids. The reasoning behind this decision was based on earlier vehicle reviews and emissions reports that appeared to contradict the Air Resources Board. Worse yet, for several reasons, the Honda Civic hybrid was one of the poorest choices management could have made.

Reduce, Reuse, Re-examine

In 2010–11, San Mateo's Civil grand jury became involved in this issue of buying only hybrid vehicles. While the Grand Jury carries no legal weight, it can demand a response within a 90–day period. The grand jury requested that Controller Tom Huening complete a follow–up report on the original audit findings and the effects of resulting policy changes. He was also asked to do a cost analysis of vehicle alternatives. What the grand jury wanted to know was the long–term implications of replacing conventional compact vehicles with pricier hybrid counterparts. Not all of Huening's findings supported preliminary grand jury data.

Huening's audit update cut through the rhetoric and parceled out the facts. It also brought a fresh dose of reality to the controversy. Huening reminded his readers that consumer purchases and predictions are always affected by changing market demands, technical improvements, and new products being brought to market. As such, comparative–analysis audits should be scheduled on a regular basis, especially for any business making large purchases.

In the San Mateo hybrid–vehicle issue, 2003–04 figures were re–examined, and new models were compared against a checklist that included miles–per–gallon, compliance with current Public Works purchasing policy, environmental goals, reliability, emissions, and ownership costs. These expenses covered purchase price, taxes, fees, fuel consumption, maintenance, repairs, and salvage value at retirement in seven years.

Low Omission Vehicles

The auditor's update report to the grand jury confirmed the

suspicions of many county residents: any cost advantage of replacing conventional fleet compact vehicles with their hybrid counterparts had long since evaporated. Over a seven–year period, a hybrid would actually cost $4,013 more to own and maintain. Take that number and multiply it by the 200 hybrids purchased during this time and the extra expense becomes a staggering $803,000. If the hybrids were compared to the Ford Fiesta, a plausible alternative, the difference became even larger, topping the million–dollar mark. Actually, this figure is still a bit low, based on the fact that during this time Toyota recalled four million vehicles to fix faulty braking systems. The Toyota Prius hybrid was on the list, further weakening its reliability rating.

The report also brought into question the expertise of those involved in the decision to purchase only Honda Civic hybrids and Toyota Prius hybrids for fleet replacements. It was noted that the Honda Insight cost almost $4,000 less than the Civic while still meeting fuel and emissions requirements. Another comparison study looked at the two fleet hybrid choices against three conventional American–made compacts: the Ford Focus, the Chevrolet Aveo, and the Chevrolet Cobalt and three conventional foreign alternatives: the Honda Fit, the Nissan Versa, and the Toyota Yaris. The hands–down winner was the Ford Focus. Its ownership costs were $6,300 less than the Civic hybrid, $5,000 less than the Prius hybrid, and $2,400 less than the Honda Insight. While the Focus listed at only 28 mpg, the difference in fuel would be less than $70.00 a year per vehicle. On the other hand, purchasing 50 Ford Focuses would save San Mateo an impressive $231,000. The audit review also suggested that retiring vehicles before 100,000 miles would increase their salvage value, another simple cost–saving measure.

An interesting controversial issue was the fact that purchasing the Honda Civic and the Toyota Prius was an exercise in sending American dollars out of the country rather than supporting the American automobile industry. This was bothersome to those concerned that local governments should set the example and be proactive in supporting a struggling American economy.

If Loving the Environment Is Wrong, I Don't Wanna Be Right

If it costs money, but doesn't promote the government's goals, it is corrupt. Citizens may agree that county government should play its part in reducing smog and greenhouse gases, but if it doesn't reduce smog or greenhouse gases and it costs more, the tactic needs to change. If an officer knows that the tactic does not meet a governmental goal but it costs money, then it isn't just corrupt, it is culpable.

Based on Auditor Huening's findings, the grand jury recommended regular cost–analysis reassessments. It questioned the financial wisdom of continuing to purchase the more expensive hybrid models. With higher purchasing costs, repealed tax credits, and emission–saving numbers too low to significantly improve the environment, it was time to say good–bye to the hybrid experiment. Somewhat wryly, the grand jury suggested, "Policy decision often requires consideration of competing priorities (in this case, cost against greenhouse emissions). Because the Board has a structured deficit, the Board and Management may need to reconsider their 'green' policy."

Despite the valuable information contained in the auditor's report, San Mateo chose to continue its policy of paying more to drive foreign hybrid vehicles. The Board dug in its heels, questioned the suggestions of the grand jury, and reiterated its position that finances were not the only consideration in this matter. In fact, the impact of the fleet's compact vehicles on the environment would be the deciding factor. As for retiring cars earlier, well, the Board would have to think about that.

Any guy who pretends he is enforcing the law and steals on his authority is a swell snake.

— Al Capone

CHAPTER 28
CHICAGO, ILLINOIS, USA

Culpable corruption thrives when accountability is non–existent or powerless. Without accountability, the door is open to conflicts of interest, poor decisions, and misappropriation of time and money that are intended for the public good. Ultimately, voters feel powerless and disenfranchised.

Chicago, former hog–slaughter capital of the world, has earned many impressive distinctions over 150 years. Unfortunately, not all of them are flattering. For more than three decades, the northern district of Illinois has captured top billing as the most corrupt area in the entire country. Such recognition is due in large measure to the infamous Chicago Political Machine, which has ruled Cook County since clear back in the mid–1880s.

Chicago's rapid population growth in the 1860s brought an unusually high level of confusion and disorder that became the perfect environment for corrupt business and government dealings. As huge immigrant populations poured into the city, acquaintances in high places became helpful job connections for brothers, cousins, nephews, best friends, and friends of best friends. Very quickly, the politics of personal obligation became the norm for Chicago and

Cook County.

Through decades of patronage, bribery, extortion, fraud, embezzlement, ghost–payrolls, and other forms of culpable corruption, these malevolent practices became the pattern of everyday business. Today, it is not unusual to catch a Chicagoan's slightly embarrassed but barely–disguised smile when he or she mentions past city or state business dealings and politics. After all, talk show hosts and commentators show no mercy when they mock the rampant crookedness that has seemed to define the character of the Windy City. However, as one astute analyst reminds us, "Corruption is not funny, and it is not free." For Chicago, the bill has averaged $300 to $500 million a year.

Does Anybody Really Know Whose Nephew This Is?

One of the key problems for both Cook County and the City of Chicago is the long–standing issue of patronage. The practice of handing out jobs and favors to political supporters, friends, and relatives thrived universally in American government until the 1880s and continues to be a problem in some areas. Today, at the highest levels, it is still expected that newly elected officials will choose high–level advisors that directly serve the official. However, at lower levels, where accountability is less direct, patronage breeds inefficiency and corruption. For most of Chicago's history, this illegal behavior has been business as usual.

Saturday in the Park District

Stories abound about employees being convicted of illegal activities and then being rehired in other positions as soon as they were released from jail. Felons often ended up working at McCormick Place or for the Chicago Park District.

Another popular but culpable practice is putting people on the payroll for non–existent positions. One such notable case involved

Marie D'Amico, daughter of a former Dean of the 39th Ward of the Chicago City Council. Ms. D'Amico was eventually convicted of receiving paychecks for no fewer than three "ghost" jobs.

The Building and Zoning Department might be considered Chicago's most reliable center for patronage hiring, bribery and corruption. After the embarrassing exposure caused by the Mirage Bar undercover operation, the mayor created the Office of Professional Review to conduct internal investigations into shakedown complaints. Just a few years later, two of that board's inspectors were indicted, along with several other employees. In 2008, half of the city's inspectors were removed for illegal favoritism. Perhaps there is a good euphemism about the Office of Professional Review that could replace "the fox guarding the henhouse."

Then there were the issues in the Fire Department. In 2009, thanks to the invention of GPS tracking systems, taxpayers learned they had been paying hundreds of thousands of dollars for falsified mileage records, and more than 80 firefighters were investigated. When employees took proficiency tests that were required for promotion, 130 were somehow "lost" and never recovered.

Both O'Hare and Midway airports have been riddled with scandals as concessions and special contracts have been consistently awarded to friends of Mayor Richard M. Daley mayor of Chicago from 1989–2011.

The list goes on and on.

Chicago did not even officially address the issue of ethics until 1987. Now, there are many ordinances and statutes that broadly criminalize corruption. But this kind of statute, even when it results in convictions, does not seem to decrease corruption.

The number of documented cases of illegal patronage, graft, bribery, extortion, fraud, and taxpayer theft is simply staggering. According to University of Illinois—Chicago professor Dick Simpson, since 1976, over 1,800 appointed or elected officials, employees, and private individuals have been convicted of public corruption in Illinois, and Chicago has been the primary scene of the crimes. Despite imposing serious consequences for corruption, there is no sign that the amount of corruption has decreased.

Beginnings

Old habits die hard, and political observers are watching with interest the closing of the Daley dynasty. In 2011, Rahm Emanuel was elected Chicago's 55th mayor. He brought with him some hopeful resources: a reputation of being his own man, the favor of the President, and strong political backing outside the city. Given these assets, he seemed equipped to pursue a new and independent way of doing city business. The 25–percent turnover of aldermen in 2011 also breathed fresh air into the system.

One of Mayor Emanuel's first appointments was an Ethics Taskforce. This was a step in the right direction, but to get rid of corruption, more was needed than mere information gathering. To be effective, Mayor Emanuel needs to embrace transparency and to spearhead a comprehensive anti–corruption strategy.

The cure for political corruption is independent auditing that leads to exposure and public accountability. There must be clear internal control rules regarding how transactions are done, including rules that require records to be kept. Periodically, an independent party must formally examine those records. Whether the examination shows that the rules have been followed or not, it must be made public. When rules are broken, there must be significant consequences, such as dismissal or criminal sanctions, even for failing to keep records. If Emanuel implements this kind of a program, the culture of corruption will begin to change.

In the past, Chicago area local governments have periodically conducted cursory internal reviews and audits, but those audits are not considered trustworthy. For example, Hay Management Group came under attack for a 2003 audit that found both Cook County and Chicago in total compliance with the Shakman decree of 1983. This ruling was designed to prevent the government from hiring workers based on their political connections. Understandably, skeptics question the validity of any Chicago audit that does not uncover even one single hiring infraction.

High quality, independent audits can eliminate corruption in every local government from small towns with small budgets to powerful cities such as Chicago with its budget of $3 billion. Using a fresh, unbiased eye, auditors uncover risks, insufficient internal controls, and inept governance. Regular, evidence–based audits allow limited resources to be allocated properly, promote ethical behavior from employees, satisfy the citizens, and increase the power and effectiveness of local government. Valuable recommendations for improvement can translate into significant dollar savings. Best of all, such long–term progress can gradually rebuild public confidence in a local government.

Keeping an audit independent and evidence–based unlocks its potential as a positive instrument of change. Independence in fact allows the auditor to operate freely without pressure or influence, but independence in appearance is also important. An agency's proven track record of integrity adds to its credibility, and thus, by association, to the credibility of the entity it audits. In Chicago and Cook County, the results of too many past audits and investigations appear to be pre–orchestrated.

Whether for a power–driven city such as Chicago or a tiny hamlet in the Adirondacks, regular audits can eliminate corruption. Hopefully, Mayor Emanuel is determined to walk this path. If so, he has much work ahead of him, but he also has an opportunity to leave a legacy much bigger than an airport or a bridge with his name on it. He can be the one that changed the culture of Chicago government.

EPILOGUE

ASPIRATIONAL ETHICS AND THE SECOND CHAIR
It's Less About Codification Than About Inspiration

GREGORY P. HAWKINS

When we give public presentations on Corruption, Ethics, or Leadership we often begin with some version of a moral hypothetical. The exercise turns out exactly the same no matter the group.

> A father takes his only child into the state school board building where she will be tested to determine if she qualifies for a very special gifted student program. Admittance is competitive and only truly gifted students will be admitted. As he approaches the test administrators, he is surprised to see his best friend. He is apparently the chair of the selection committee. His friend greets him very warmly and tells him not to worry, his daughter will get into the program. Both men understand the implication.

Most people will say that it is wrong for the administrator to treat his friend's daughter differently from other applicants. In many groups, there will be some who feel so strongly that it is wrong that they speak out without prompting. Yet even those who speak out will hesitate to call it "evil."

Morals are the basic internal principles that inform and govern a person's view of right and wrong, good and evil. Although morals are almost a universal force, they can be diverse in their application and definition–almost as diverse as individuals are from one another. This diversity is illustrated as we add to our hypothetical.

The facts added do not change the action itself, but they do change the moral context by emphasizing a competing virtue.

What if the administrator and his friend were not merely lifelong friends, but they fought together in the war, side–by–side, depending on one another for their life? What if the father had actually, and rather dramatically, saved the administrator's life? What if the father had been wounded in his heroic effort? What if the wound had left him unable to father another child? What if he was left a paraplegic, forever reliant on a wheelchair for his mobility? As we proceed with each, "what if," more and more people begin to rethink their opinion. Often, the ones who felt so strongly about the wrongness of the administrator's actions will be among the first to change their view.

As each group looks around the room at what they thought was a homogenous group, they begin to realize that questions of right and wrong, good and evil, even in their very own analysis, sometimes take real thought to resolve. Sometimes the questions involve good and good, right and right. Which is more important, equality or loyalty? In the abstract, this question is challenging, but it can become quite difficult if it is a question one faces in their own life. Which is the greater good, fairness in testing and equality of school programs, or loyalty and honoring life–changing sacrifice? We have discovered that individual resolution of this issue sometimes turns on the person's life experience. For example, a veteran of combat often sees the question differently than does a president of the PTA. When the person is both a combat veteran and the president of the PTA, the question becomes intense.

Let's turn from the question of morals to the question of ethics. If we were to ask 100 ethicists what the definition of ethics is, we may well receive 147 different answers. For our purposes, we will use the working definition that "ethics are one's discretionary behavior in relation to morals." Some ethicists use the term ethics to mean the rules crafted by others to be applied to someone else's moral conduct. We will refer to the creation of someone else's rules as the "codification of ethics." We will define codification as simply, "the creation of an organized set of rules that if violated have a negative consequence to the violator."

Although intended to improve the moral climate, the codification of ethics tends to decrease ethical choices. We will briefly discuss five reasons why ethical choices decrease when ethics are codified.

First is the concept of legal moralism. If the conduct is not prohibited in the code of ethics, then, by definition, it is permitted conduct. In other words, license is given to engage in conduct not specifically prohibited by the code. This is not to say that codification of ethics results in absolute legal moralism to every person in every circumstance. The question of whether the conduct is right or wrong, good or evil, for some, can simply be set aside. The rules themselves determine the right and wrong of behavior. Discretion can become irrelevant. This results in less ethical behavior. To avoid this result, continuing codification is required until all conduct that is perceived as bad is prohibited. The code must be exhaustive–a nearly impossible task.

Second, because violation of the code results in negative consequences, whenever the code is applied to an individual, that individual resists its application. The person must say, "I did not do it," or "That rule does not apply to me," or "You are reading the code incorrectly," or a multitude of variations on this theme. Any individual to whom the code applies, now or in the future, naturally and even subconsciously resists the code. Because the individual resists the application of the code, the rules lose their ability to affect the person's choices in relation to morals positively. Codification may result in nearly universal resistance by those who are governed.

Third, when negative consequences are threatened, a lawyer—an expert dedicated to exploiting ambiguities in the law and its application to specific facts—is invited to participate in the ensuing battle. Yes, it will be a battle, because almost no one willingly submits to his behavior being characterized as bad, or as wrong and certainly not as evil. The lawyer's job is to defend her client, not to promote generalized ethical behavior. The lawyer will find the ambiguities in the code being applied, as well as ambiguities in the underlying facts. In time, often a very short time, the code becomes diluted, its benefits reduced.

This dilution takes us to a fourth problem of codification. Like legal moralism, dilution requires additions to the code—more codification. Dilution requires a codification that is tighter in its application and more exhaustive, which in turn will require more lawyers, and round and round and round we go.

Fifth, codification does not promote good behavior. At its best, codification can only limit bad behavior.

As a result of these and other effects, codification by its nature results in less ethical behavior. This is a significant idea and bears repeating: rules that take away discretion, choices, about moral behavior result in less ethical behavior because ethics is about discretionary behavior in relation to morals–it is about choices.

Despite the problems with the codification of ethics, no one is advocating that we do away with it. Codification of ethics will always be a part of our modern world.

In 1100 AD there were about 50 million people inhabiting our planet. In the 1820s we reached our first billion. In the 1920s, 100 years later, we reached our second billion. In January of 2013 we reached 7 billion. In 2013, there were also 206 nation−states in the world. Each country represents a somewhat, if not a radically different set of laws, rules, and principles people apply when governing their lives, grounded in numerous cultural, religious, ethnic, and racial perspectives of right and wrong, good and evil. Twenty–eight percent of the world is Christian, twenty–two percent Muslim, fifteen percent Hindu, eight and half percent Buddhists, fourteen percent are found in the "other religions" category, and twelve percent are categorized as nonreligious. Under each general heading there is a vast number of denominations or sects. For example, there are over 1500 different Christian sects or faith groups. And even within a group espousing the same morals, individuals apply them differently to real life circumstances.

Advances in technology are bringing the earth's seven billion diverse inhabitants into contact with each other more and more frequently. We bump into each other, over and over again. The innumerable interactions mean people will witness more behavior that is wrong or evil. Therefore, there will be a growing cry, "There ought to be a law!"

This continuing call for codification of ethics–local, national or international–happens in many contexts: corporate, governmental, or across a profession or industry. This is the reality when so many people have such easy access to one another.

However, as discussed, codification alone will not result in more good behavior. We cannot expect that codification will increase good behavior nor can we choose simply not to codify. Nevertheless, we cannot abandon our desire to increase good behavior. Nor can we abandon our confidence that, given the opportunity, most people will exercise their discretion, their choices in relation to morals, positively. This brings us to the Second Chair.

Tom Robinson was a black man accused of raping and beating a white woman in "Jim Crow" Alabama in the 1930's.

To put it mildly, due process and trial by a jury of one's peers were not the popular approach to resolve such issues in the rural South at that time. There were 4,742 lynchings in America from 1882 to 1964. Alabama accounted for 347 of these and the South at large over 3,130. Rape, attempted rape, and insult to a white person accounted for 1,285, about 27 percent of these lynchings. A black man accused of one of these crimes could reasonably expect to die without due process of law.

Tom Robinson was not destined for trial. He was jailed and charged. The local judge asked the best–liked, most respected lawyer in Maycomb County to represent Tom in this lost cause—Atticus Finch. You know the rest of the story. Harper Lee's novel *To Kill a Mockingbird* won a Pulitzer Prize. It was made into a movie and Gregory Peck won the Academy Award for his portrayal of Atticus Finch. In 2003 the American Film Institute named Atticus Finch the number one hero in 100 years of film, ahead of Indiana Jones and James Bond. But what you do not know is that an examination of this story, and thousands of others, illustrates well the principle of the Second Chair.

Harper Lee wrote *To Kill a Mockingbird* in 1960, just as the modern civil rights movement really began to heat up. She used Atticus's young daughter, Scout, as the voice to teach us.

It was a Sunday night and word came to Atticus that the locals were going to the jail to administer justice. Atticus went to the jail, set up a chair and a small living room lamp he'd brought with him and sat outside the jail reading and waiting. Unbeknownst to Atticus, his son, Jem, Scout, and their friend Dill had followed him and were hiding behind a bush, watching.

Soon local justice arrived in the form of cars filled with angry and determined southern white men. Scout didn't recognize any of them. The men got out of their cars and told Atticus to leave. The moment got tense. Scout and the boys busted out from hiding and ran to Atticus. Scout was surprised at the fear that flashed across Atticus's face at seeing the children. Scout did not understand what was happening as she looked again at the crowd for a familiar face. Harsh words were spoken telling Atticus to send the children home. Jem refused to go, sensing the danger to Atticus.

Finally, Scout recognized someone in the crowd. It was Walter Cunningham, a client of Atticus. She said, "Hey, Mr. Cunningham." He pretended not to hear her.

She began a solo, innocent dialogue with him about his work with Atticus, about school, about his son Walter, and so on. Mr. Cunningham tried to ignore her and eventually she simply said, "Tell him hey for me, won't you?" The scene remained tense and Scout was confused. She finally asked, "What's the matter?"

Mr. Cunningham squatted down and took Scout by the shoulders and said, "I'll tell him you said hey, little lady." And then he stood and said, "Let's go boys." Tom Robinson would live, at least for that Sunday night.

In the 1950s Solomon E. Asch, of Swarthmore College, conducted an unusual psychology experiment. Although this experiment is the inspiration for what follows, we are not relying upon its purposes, findings, or applications. Rather, the experiment is merely the catalyst of thought to pursue our own applications. The participants in the experiment were informed that it was a visual perception experiment. It was not.

Six people are placed in chairs. Diagrams of lines are shown to them. On the left is shown a line of certain length. On the right are three lines of different lengths, one of which matches exactly the line on the left. The correct choice is clear and obvious.

The only person actually being tested is the person in the Fifth Chair; everyone else is a co–conspirator. When the test begins, chairs 1–4 and 6 purposely identify the wrong line as the correct match. If the correct answer is "B," then they all say "A." The Fifth Chair identifies the obviously correct line as the match. "It's B."

The co–conspirators, subtly at first, and then more directly, ridicule the Fifth Chair for choosing the "wrong" line. As the participants are shown set after set of lines, eventually, and often quite quickly, the Fifth Chair begins to give the wrong answer, the same as the co–conspirators, even though the correct answer is obvious.

Then the experiment changes. The person in the Second Chair begins to give the correct answer. Now, the Fifth Chair almost always gives the correct answer, too. With the voice of the Second Chair added, the Fifth Chair is not persuaded by the taunts of the others to join them in giving the wrong answer. The Fifth Chair gives what he knows is the correct answer. "It's B."

This experiment is the backdrop for what follows. Many people sit in the Fifth Chair. The truth of something seems obvious: this line is the same length as line "B." But the multitude of voices saying, shouting, sometimes demanding, that the correct answer is "A" creates the environment in which the Fifth Chair finds it compelling to remain quiet or even agree with the demanding but wrong voices.

When the Second Chair steps up and says, "It's B," when the Second Chair communicates the truth about what the Fifth Chair sees, powerful things happen.

In our earlier retelling of the jail scene from *To Kill a Mockingbird*, Scout unknowingly occupies the Second Chair and Walter Cunningham the Fifth Chair. Harper Lee artfully illustrated the power of Scout's innocent little voice helping Walter choose what, to Harper Lee, 1960 America, and us today, was the obvious—justice does not come by a vigilante rope in the dark of night. The mob around him was saying, "It's A," "Let's lynch this man." But Scout said to Walter, "It's B," and Walter's burden of choice was lifted for a moment and he was able to act.

Let's follow the story just a bit further. Tom Robinson goes on trial. Atticus presents evidence that to the reader, and to Atticus's son, Jem, makes it absolutely clear that Tom Robinson could not have beaten the girl. Tom's left arm had been permanently damaged beyond use when he was a boy. He was physically unable to strike her on the side of her body where the evidence indicated she was beaten. However, the girl's father was left handed and known to have a very bad temper. Further, no medical evidence was introduced that showed the girl was ever raped.

Jem was elated until the verdict came. After several hours of deliberation the jury found Tom Robinson guilty. Jem was crushed at the obvious injustice. Atticus explained to the distraught Jem that a jury would usually take only a few minutes to convict Tom—a black man accused of raping a white woman. But this jury took hours.

> "You might like to know that there was one fellow who took considerable wearing down—in the beginning he was rarin' for an outright acquittal."
>
> "Who?" Jem was astonished.
>
> Atticus's eyes twinkled. "It's not for me to say, but I'll tell you this much. He was one of your Old Sarum friends…"
>
> "One of the Cunninghams?" Jem yelped. "One of – I didn't recognize any of 'em…you're jokin." He looked at Atticus from the corners of his eyes.
>
> "One of their connections. On a hunch, I didn't strike him. Just on a hunch. Could've, but I didn't."
>
> "Golly Moses," Jem said reverently. "One minute they're tryin' to kill him and the next they're tryin' to turn him loose"…
>
> Atticus said… "it took a thunderbolt plus another Cunningham to make one of them change his mind. If we'd had two of that crowd, we'd've had a hung jury."

> Jem said slowly, "you mean you actually put on the jury a man who wanted to kill you the night before? How could you take such a risk, Atticus, how could you?" (*To Kill a Mockingbird,* Grand Central Publishing, Hachette Book Group, Inc., April 2010 © 1960 Harper Lee, pages 297, 298.)

Scout, the unknowing Second Chair, speaks to Walter Cunningham, the unknowing Fifth Chair, "Hey Mr. Cunningham." Within seconds Walter says, "Let's go," and other Fifth Chair Cunninghams are lastingly affected. One of them becomes a Fifth Chair himself in the jury room, "rarin' for an acquittal." If only he'd had a Second Chair! "If we'd had two of that crowd, we'd've had a hung jury." A hung jury in 1930's segregated, Jim Crow, Alabama with a black man accused of rape.

Let's look at another Second Chair experience. It was August 28, 1963. Hundreds of thousands had gathered on the National Mall in Washington, D.C. facing the Lincoln Memorial. Fifteen speakers were scheduled to speak. The last speaker had been cautioned by his advisers, by the event organizer, and even by the Kennedy Administration, to be careful. It's a big stage. Don't cause problems. The speech he was to give was written by others. It was well–crafted and very persuasive. Yet compared to others he had given, it was a bit bland. He had some thoughts he wanted to share and was burdened by whether or not to share them despite the cautions. Toward the end of his prepared remarks, as he struggled whether or not to share these thoughts, a friend standing several rows behind him, Mahalia Jackson, the well–known singer, yelled out, "Tell them about the dream, Martin."

Martin Luther King, Jr. quietly slid the prepared remarks to the side and calmly and carefully said, "I have a dream." The rest is history. No other speaker, no other remarks are remembered from that day. The speech itself, the written text of which contains no reference to the dream, still echoes through time. King sat burdened in the Fifth Chair with close advisers and important people occupying the

First Chair. He wants to tell it; he thinks it's right; he thinks it will make a difference. They tell him he is wrong; don't cause problems; stick to the written speech. Mahalia Jackson, sitting in the Second Chair, reaches out with just a few words and, for a moment only, lifts King's Fifth Chair burden–tell them about the dream, Martin. Mahalia Jackson said to Martin Luther King, Jr., "It's B."

Another scene: it is 1804 and thirty–two men and a Shoshone woman drag themselves into a Nez Perce village at the western edge of the Bitterroot Mountains. The village feeds the nearly starved group. But so rich is the food that without exception they are sick and further weakened. With them they have hundreds of firearms, ammunition and powder. The Nez Perce are a small tribe in the midst of much stronger tribes.

A council of elders discusses what should be done. Strong voices speak to kill them and take their weapons. The weapons could very well change the balance of power among the tribes. Other voices speak to befriend them and nurse them to health. After all, men with such weapons are better friends than enemies and surely will trade for more weapons if befriended. The Council makes its decision: kill them while they are defenseless.

A woman lying in her deathbed within hearing of the Council rises with difficulty and joins the circle of elders. Her unexpected presence, her deathly appearance, and the legend of her life command the attention of the elders. Her name is Watkuweis which means, "Returned from a Far Country." She had been kidnapped at 13 by a neighboring tribe and traded from tribe to tribe, in time being taken 1800 miles to the east. Her legend chronicles her deprivation and abuse. Eventually she is helped to escape by some white settlers in the Great Lakes area and given a few supplies. Miraculously and at great cost, she makes it back to her tribe. She now stands before the tribal Council and simply says, "Men like these were good to me, do them no hurt." Watkuweis says to the Council, "It's B" and the Council changes its decision.

Among those saved that day were Meriwether Lewis and William Clark. The Shoshone woman was Sacagawea. The Lewis and Clark expedition mapped, surveyed and explored 820,000 square miles of uncharted territory. The expedition was the tipping point for the United States' expansion. But for the word of a dying woman, sitting in the Second Chair, saying to some on the Council sitting in the Fifth Chair, "It's B," the great and historically important contributions by Lewis and Clark would have ended abruptly on the western edge of the Bitterroot Mountains.

Jackie Robinson sat in the Fifth Chair. In fact, he was specifically selected and purposely placed in the Fifth Chair by Branch Rickey, general manager of the Brooklyn Dodgers. Because of his moral backbone, his controlled temper, and his athletic ability, Jackie was the perfect choice. Many times the First Chair piled on ridicule, racial epithets, and even death threats. Jackie felt alone. Once the manager of the Philadelphia Phillies, Ben Chapman, occupying the First Chair, verbally beat Jackie nearly to explosive anger while Jackie was at bat. He said things that today would be outrageous in public or private.

Jackie was at the point of breaking and almost walked over to Chapman to brain him with the bat. But one of Robinson's teammates, Eddie Stanky, stepped out of the dugout, walked over to Chapman and said, in substance, "Stop it. You are wrong." The comments had little effect on Chapman, but they had a powerful effect on Robinson. Robinson's teammate sat in the Second Chair at a critical time for Jackie, who carried the burden of a terrible Fifth Chair dilemma: do I brain Chapman or do I hold my peace? Robinson's teammate lifted that burden, for just a moment, and said to Jackie, "It's B."

Jackie was still in the Fifth Chair on another field in Cincinnati. Pee Wee Reese, also a teammate of Robinson, sat in the Second Chair. The people in the First Chair were family and friends of Pee

Wee from across the Ohio River in Kentucky. As Jackie took the field, Pee Wee's family began to throw verbal spears at Jackie, not too different from those of Ben Chapman. Pee Wee walked across the field to where Jackie stood and in the presence of all, his family included, simply put his arm around Jackie and began to talk. Once more, a teammate sat in the Second Chair and said to Jackie, "It's B."

But, that's not the end of the story. In the stands were young nephews of Pee Wee. Unbeknownst to Pee Wee, they were also in the Fifth Chair. They did not believe the terrible things the adult family members were saying; they had a choice to make. Pee Wee, by simply putting his arm around Jackie, said loud and clear, "It's B." They chose not to participate in their elder's efforts to intimidate Jackie.

We refer to these experiences as Aspirational Ethics and the Second Chair. Ethics are discretionary behaviors in relationship to morals. Ethics are about the choices we make in relation to how we see right and wrong, good and evil. Codification can limit bad behavior, but as discussed, more and more codification is required to be effective. Codification does not encourage good behavior and tends to result in less overall ethical behavior—fewer choices in relationship to right and wrong, good and evil.

The vast majority of people when asked, "Are you good?," will hesitate to say, "Yes." Nevertheless, when asked, "Do you want to be good?," most say "Yes," without much prodding. A "Yes" answer is even more forthcoming when asked, "Do you want to do good?" It is rare, indeed, for someone to actually aspire to be evil or to do evil.

Why? Why do most people readily declare that they want to do good? David, before he became king, before he slew Goliath, said to his brother, Eliab, "is there not a cause," is there not a reason I am at this place, at this time?

Almost everyone feels deep inside themselves, purpose. Sometimes the feeling of purpose can get overshadowed by the moment or even by a lifetime of moments. But just like David of old—we have purpose, there is a cause, a reason for us being in the places we find ourselves, interacting with the people with whom we are interacting.

Sometimes, even very often, the reason is to sit in the Second Chair and say to the Fifth Chair, whose purpose is temporarily overshadowed by First Chair voices, "It's B." and when we do, just like a tuning fork resonates with the piano string, our Second Chair voice resonates with truth and purpose of the Fifth Chair and powerful things happen.

Aspirational Ethics and the Second Chair encourages awareness and choices in relationship to morals. It is always the Fifth Chair that has the power and carries the burden of decision. We all sit in the Fifth Chair at times. Unfortunately, we may sometimes sit in the First Chair and get it totally wrong. But we can aspire to sit in the Second Chair. We can actively look for those sitting in the Fifth Chair whose choices are burdened with the pounding voices of those sitting in the First Chair. Our aspiration does not require heroic labors; it may be as simple as a thumbs-up or a pat on the back. The Second Chair need only communicate to the Fifth Chair, you are seeing it right, "It's B."

While we often struggle with our own Fifth Chair choices, we can aspire to sit in the Second Chair every time the opportunity arises. Aspirational Ethics and the Second Chair is about the moment. History, individual history and collective history, is about critical moments. We never know when the moment will come or how critical the moment may be. Nevertheless, we can look for and be aware of those in the Fifth Chair. We can recognize the burden placed on them by the multitude of First Chair voices. We can lift that burden, even if it is only for a moment, and inspire the choice to do good by our reaffirming voice, "It's B." And, when we do, powerful things ***will*** happen!

ACKNOWLEDGEMENTS

We are grateful to many people for helping us create this work. Michael Anderson and Michael Chabries helped us learn, evaluate, and expand many of the concepts that we discuss. Wordsmiths K.J. McElrath, John Regan, and Janet Perigo helped us turn technical audit reports into interesting stories. Claude Hawkins always provides a critical eye and pointed suggestions that improve the quality of our work. Marci Wahlquist's editing skills enhance our efforts and save us from much embarrassment. Our children motivate us by their love and the promise of their future to actively seek a better world. Our wives Arlene and Diana lift our burdens every day, give us the most wonderful reasons to live and work, and bring joy to an often challenging world. Lastly, and most importantly, we express our deepest gratitude to Him to whom we owe all gratitude.

ABOUT THE AUTHORS

Gregory P. Hawkins and Lonn Litchfield are speakers, writers and lawyers. Gregory P. Hawkins was the elected Salt Lake County Auditor from 2011 through 2014. Lonn Litchfield was Greg's Chief Deputy in the Auditor's office. Greg has thirty years of trial experience and has published and spoken on a diverse array of topics. Lonn has two law degrees, one from the London School of Economics and spent most of his practice years in the court room. Together they make a good lawyer. Both have been intensely interested in public policy, law, government and liberty from their youth. Since their meeting two decades ago, they have labored on numerous projects together, practiced law together, politicked together, fought shoulder to shoulder, laughed, argued, cried, prayed, inspired, aspired and laughed some more.

CPSIA information can be obtained at www.ICGtesting.com
Printed in the USA
BVOW03s2031220714

360001BV00006B/23/P